REFLECTIONS ON THE CHURCH

CARLO CARDINAL MARTINI

REFLECTIONS ON THE CHURCH

Meditations on Vatican II

VERITAS

Published 1987 by
Veritas Publications
7-8 Lower Abbey Street
Dublin 1

Italian language edition published 1986 by
Edizioni Piemme
15033 Casale Monferrato
Italy

ISBN 1 85390 000 1

Translation: Luke Griffin
Cover design: Eddie McManus
Typesetting: Printset & Design Ltd, Dublin
Printed in the Republic of Ireland by
Mount Salus Press Ltd, Dublin

CONTENTS

INTRODUCTION

With some trepidation we begin our School of Prayer which we hope will be a time of shared contemplative silence for all of us.

This is a new venture both for me and for you. Psalm 27 may help us to get into the spirit of the meeting. This psalm can be divided into two parts.

The first part (1-6) could be called *a crisis-free period of euphoria.* To the one praying all seems straightforward and clear; 'whom shall I fear?' ... 'of whom shall I be afraid?'. It is the adversaries who shall stumble and fall. 'Though a host encamp against me, my heart shall not fear ...'

The psalmist's experience of God seems to make him invincible — dwelling in the house of the Lord and beholding his beauty.

Then suddenly something happens. The second part of the psalm begins with verse 7. The same man who was sincere in his joy at living near the house of the Lord and the feeling of security this gave him, now begins to experience anguish and fear. This second phase might be called *the storm.* 'Hear O Lord when I cry aloud ... hide not thy face from me ... forsake me not ...' even though others may have forsaken me. Here we have the experience of one who senses that all that was good and comforting in his thought about God is now slipping away. It is precisely at this moment of trial that his prayer becomes more pure and more insistent. 'Teach me thy way ... give me not up to the will of my adversaries ...' He regains his composure. 'I believe that I shall see the goodness of the Lord ... Wait for the Lord, be strong ...'

His confidence is all the greater for having passed through the crisis of the storm.

Who recites this psalm? In the history of salvation, apart from those who originally lived through this experience personally, the *psalm is recited by Jesus*. It could be said that the first part is Jesus' prayer on the mount of the Transfiguration; the second part is his prayer in the Garden of Gethsemane, where he suffered agony, anxiety and fear.

Then again the psalm is recited by the Church in its moments of euphoria as during the years when Vatican II was in session when the first part of the psalm was an expression of the experience of the Church. In the more sombre post-conciliar period the Church experiences the storm and the fear, the second part of the psalm.

The psalm is therefore Jesus' prayer and the prayer of the Church with Jesus. Now I would like you to pray Psalm 27 not so much as your own personal prayer but rather as the prayer of your parish: try to relive in prayer the moments of joy and anguish of your parish community; live them with the Church and with Jesus in one simple prayer ascending to the Father.

Our meetings here on the first Thursdays are primarily for members of parish pastoral councils. My main aim is to help you to deepen your sense of responsibility for the Church and to develop an ever sharper ecclesial sense. On these two will depend your ability to be a constructive presence in pastoral councils and in all the other initiatives which express and build up the community according to the divine model for the Church. A responsible presence means contributing to the upbuilding of the diocesan community of which parishes are the parts; it is not a matter of engaging in polemic or mere discussion. I therefore perceive the role and function of these meetings as providing help in the task of practical reflection on the divine model of the Church so that each participant can express and outline this experience in parish councils and in the community. I attach so much importance to these meetings that I have been willing to leave aside for the moment my usual prayer meetings with our young adults in order to concentrate my energies and those of the Catholic Action groups on this reflective task.

Those of you who are not members of parish pastoral councils should nevertheless feel that you are being challenged not merely as individuals but rather as having co-responsibility for the building up of the local Church.

In order to reflect on the divine model of the Church we will listen to the word of God, convinced that it will teach us things hitherto unknown to us and make us see realities of which we were previously unaware.

We will base ourselves on the New Testament and on the documents of Vatican II. This is a worthy way of celebrating the twentieth anniversary of the Council, in accordance with the wishes of the Holy Father. This way too we hope to grasp the emphasis on the theme of Church about which Vatican II has said so much.

This evening we will concentrate on the first document approved by the Council in 1964 — the Constitution on the Liturgy which speaks of the Church that prays.

The Church that prays

In the texts of the New Testament and of the Constitution on the Liturgy *(Sacrosanctum Concilium — SC)*, the Church is shown as a Church that prays.

(1) *When has the Church prayed and when has it been seen to pray?* Right from the very beginning. In Acts 2:42-46 we have the first historical description of the Church.

A typical day in the life of the early community is described, from nine in the morning until nightfall, and at the end of the account we find: 'And they devoted themselves to the Apostles' teaching and fellowship, to the breaking of the bread (Eucharist) and to the prayers ... and day by day attending the Temple ... praising God'.

Right from the beginning, then, the Church is at prayer. And the Church always prays. If you re-read Acts you will find a mention of prayer in each of its twenty-eight chapters. This is meant to underline the fact that to be in prayer is a constant and permanent characteristic of the Church. For this very reason the document *Sacrosanctum Concilium* repeats the quotation from Acts *(2:41-42. 47)* and goes on to say. 'From that time the Church has never failed to assemble for the celebration of the paschal mystery.' From the first Pentecost to this very day in November 1985 the Church has always assembled in prayer. There has never been a day, a time when the Church ceased to pray.

(2) *How has the Church prayed, how does it pray?* It has prayed like Christ. The words of Luke's description of the Transfiguration

11

come to mind: 'And as he was praying, the appearance of his countenance became altered and his garment became dazzling white' (cf Luke 9:28-35). When he prayed Jesus as it were changed his everyday appearance and became a shining luminous figure. I underline this incident in order to understand how the Church prays — like *Christ, transfiguring itself.*

Let us examine this notion in more depth. When the Church prays, especially when it prays as a visible community, as for example when celebrating the Eucharist, it moves out of the appearance and conditions of everyday life. Prayer is an action which takes place at a different level from other events. People do not simply come together to recite fine formulas, to listen to interesting words or to sing; rather we are dealing with ecstasy — a going out of ourselves — with transfiguration, with self-forgetfulness.

Any liturgy is poor if it is not in some way ecstatic. Hence in visible, tangible ways the Church indicates that when it is at prayer it is carrying out an activity that differs from many others: the priest is robed in sacred vestments, the altar is tastefully prepared, incense is used and so on ... The Church is living a divine mystery, we are entering the sphere of the divine *with* and *like* Christ.

How many times have I not experienced during a liturgical celebration that people have managed to forget themselves, losing even the desire of having at all costs 'a fine liturgy': they then began to lose themselves in God, in the Crucified, in the inexpressible mystery of the Trinity; they allowed themselves to be grasped through signs by the divine presence.

On the other hand I have also had an almost physical sense that during certain liturgies the congregation remained preoccupied with itself, either as individuals or as a group: people remained divided; they never took off and their prayer seemed to fall back on them.

The prayer of the Church then is a type of ecstasy, of transfiguration: The liturgical symbols, vestments, gestures and words are all aids to a living experience of the divine.

Two objections
Two immediate objections have to be faced. *The first:* Is not this understanding of the prayer of the Church some kind of

alienation, a form of estrangement from daily life?

The answer is simple: In order to get a proper perspective on the realities of daily life it is necessary to be able to rise above them. The person who is not in the control tower cannot grasp what is happening on the runways!

The ecstatic movement to which the liturgy draws us, to which we are drawn by the crucified eucharistic Christ, is our best guarantee of level-headedness in our everyday activity, of an ability to make proper value judgements about material things and to attribute importance only to things that are really important. To live a moment of self-forgetfulness, of entry into the divine fire, helps us to acquire the viewpoint of God, the attitude of Christ.

The Church's transfiguration in prayer is not therefore alienation but is a door through which we gain entry to the truth of things and which allows us to see them from God's point of view.

The second: How can we do this given the frailty of our nature and the thousand and one preoccupations, distractions and frivolities that weigh us down?

There are two answers to this:

(a) The first we find in the letter to the Hebrews: 'In the days of his flesh Jesus offered up prayers and supplications with loud cries and tears ...' *(Heb 5:7)*. The answer lies in the tears of Jesus and in the heartfelt cry of Psalm 27 which we make our own: 'Hide not thy face from me ... turn not thy servant away in anger ... forsake me not ... lead me on a level path ... give me not up to the will of my adversaries'.

   Prayer is itself a recognition of our own frailty, a confession to God of our inability: Though he had not sinned, Jesus wanted to share our poverty and prayed with humility, distress and tears. The liturgy is full of sentiments of heartfelt distress, contrition, and sorrow. 'Create in me a clean heart, O God, and put a new and right spirit within me' (cf. Psalm 51, the Miserere). The Mass itself begins with the prayer, 'You came to call sinners, Lord have mercy'. Thus, liturgy responds to our confession of our weakness and powerlessness.

(b) The second answer is that the Church inserts our poverty into the prayer of Christ. It is he whom we meet, and who

13

raises us up when we pray. We are drawn by his cross, by its mystery of adoration and offering. We become one with him. In this respect I recall my pastoral letter (*I will draw all to myself*) in preparation for the Eucharistic Congress. We are drawn into the offering of the crucified Christ and become part of him through the Eucharist.

'In fact — *Sacrosanctum Concilium* states — in this most wonderful work ... Christ always associates the Church, his most beloved spouse, with himself. He is present in the sacrifice of the Mass .. he is present through his power in the sacraments .. he is present in his word ... he is present when the Church prays and praises .. he is always present in the Church'.

Christ, taking us into himself, releases us from the prison of our own mediocrity and leads us to share in the divine largesse of what is in his heart.

Questions for us

We have said that the Church has prayed from *the beginning* and *always* prays. It prays like Christ and is transfigured. We can put questions to the members of the Council:

Firstly, how do we treat the opening prayers at parish meetings? I know of the praiseworthy practice in some parishes of beginning meetings with the recital of Vespers or Compline or by reciting a psalm. Is this prayer merely to await the arrival of latecomers? Or is it an effort to penetrate that mystery which, during the course of reflection, we must later make visible in a practical way?

Secondly, what initiatives are taken in our parish to facilitate and sustain a certain continuity of prayer among the faithful? What are the annual, monthly or weekly events which seek to underline a constant rhythm of prayer whether in church or in the home?

Thirdly, to what degree is our prayer, even our personal prayer, ecstatic? By ecstasy I mean forgetting myself, my own and others heaviness (my neighbour does this-and-that wrong ...!). I mean a rising above daily banality and an entering into the dynamic rhythm of the mystery of God. What impedes this ecstatic experience during our personal prayer, and in our prayer in church, in the parish, during Mass and other liturgical celebrations?

14

Are there areas of sloth, carelessness, lack of enthusiasm? Do you arrive late for Mass? When one is aware of constant shuffling, of people coming late, the ecstatic moment crumbles away as our attention wanders to see who has come, who hasn't a place, who pushes themselves to the front! Liturgical prayer requires the cooperation of all concerned and this is not achieved without a major effort. Or perhaps some of the liturgical group are careless; perhaps the choir is ill-prepared!

Finally, what is the penitential quality of my personal prayer? Let us think of Christ who prayed *with tears.*

Am I like the Pharisee who feels that things were in order in his life, or am I like the publican who asks the Lord to be merciful to him? Do I regularly avail myself of the Sacrament of Penance, thereby living the penitential spirit of the liturgy and promoting a correct attitude towards the Eucharist? Frequently, personal prayer and, indeed, community prayer fails to take off and remains barren, taxis on the ground, never gaining height, because it is not nourished by the necessary penitential attitude which makes us recognise our own unworthiness to stand in the presence of God, our inability to utter words that ring true, our need to see his face. 'Show me your face O Lord, your face O Lord do I seek'.

And trying to make this prayer our own we can now begin our adoration of the Eucharist.

1

THE CHURCH IN PRAYER

(Psalm 27)
The Lord is my light and my salvation;
* whom shall I fear?*
The Lord is the stronghold of my life;
* of whom shall I be afraid?*

When evildoers assail me,
* uttering slanders against me,*
my adversaries and foes,
* they shall stumble and fall.*

Though a host encamp against me,
* my heart shall not fear;*
though war arise against me,
* yet I will be confident.*

One thing have I asked of the Lord,
* that will I seek after;*
that I may dwell in the house of the Lord
* all the days of my life,*
to behold the beauty of the Lord,
* and to inquire in his temple.*

For he will hide me in his shelter
* in the day of trouble;*
he will conceal me under the cover of his tent,
* he will set me high upon a rock.*

And now my head shall be lifted up
* above my enemies round about me;*

and I will offer in his tent
  sacrifices with shouts of joy;
I will sing and make melody to the Lord.

Hear, O Lord, when I cry aloud,
  be gracious to me and answer me!
Thou hast said, 'Seek ye my face.'
  My heart says to thee,
'Thy face, Lord, do I seek.'
  Hide not thy face from me.

Turn not thy servant away in anger,
  thou who hast been my help.
Cast me not off, forsake me not,
  O God of my salvation!
For my father and my mother have forsaken me,
  but the Lord will take me up.

Teach me thy way, O Lord;
  and lead me on a level path because of my enemies.
Give me not up to the will of my adversaries;
  for false witnesses have risen against me,
  and they breathe out violence.

I believe that I shall see the goodness of the Lord
  in the land of the living!

Wait for the Lord;
  be strong, and let your heart take courage;
  yea, wait for the Lord!

From Luke's Gospel *(9:28-35)*

Now about eight days after those sayings he took with him Peter and John and James, and went up on the mountain to pray. And as he was praying the appearance of his countenance was altered and his raiment became dazzling white. And behold, two men talked with him, Moses and Elijah, who appeared in glory and spoke of his departure which he was to accomplish in Jerusalem. Now Peter and those who were with him were heavy with sleep but kept awake, and they saw his glory and the two men who stood with him. And as the men were parting from him Peter said to Jesus, 'Master, it is well that we are here; let us make three booths, one for you and one for Moses and one for Elijah' — not knowing what he said. As he said this, a cloud came and overshadowed them; and they were afraid

*as they entered the cloud. And a voice came out of the cloud saying 'This
is my Son, my Chosen, listen to him!'*

From the Letter to the Hebrews *(5:7-10)*
*In the days of his flesh, Jesus offered up prayers and supplications, with
loud cries and tears, to him who was able to save him from death, and
he was heard for his godly fear. Although he was a Son, he learned obedience
through what he suffered, and being made perfect he became the source
of eternal salvation to all who obey him, being designated by God a high
priest after the order of Melchizedek.*

From the Acts of the Apostles *(2:42-46)*
*And they devoted themselves to the apostles' teaching and fellowship, to
the breaking of bread and the prayers. And fear came upon every soul;
and many wonders and signs were done through the apostles. And all who
believed were together and had all things in common; and they sold their
possessions and goods and distributed them to all as any had need. And
day by day, attending the temple together and breaking bread in their homes,
they partook of food with glad and generous hearts, praising God and having
favour with all the people.*

From the Constitution on Sacred Liturgy, *Sacrosanctum Concilium* *(nn. 6-8)*
*That was why on the very day of Pentecost when the Church appeared
before the world those 'who received the word' of Peter 'were baptised'.
And 'they continued steadfastly in the teaching of the apostles and in the
communion of the breaking of bread and in prayers ... praising God and
being in favour with all the people' (Acts 2:41-47). From that time onward
the Church has never failed to come together to celebrate the paschal mystery,
reading those things 'which were in all the scriptures concerning him' (Lk
24:27) celebrating the Eucharist in which the victory and triumph of his
death are again made present, and at the same time giving thanks to God
for his inexpressible gift (2 Cor 9:15) in Jesus Christ, 'in praise of his
glory' (Eph 1:12) through the power of the Holy Spirit.*

*To accomplish so great a work Christ is always present in his Church,
especially in her liturgical celebrations. He is present in the sacrifice of
the Mass not only in the person of his minister, the same now offering,
through the ministry of priests, who formerly offered himself on the cross,
but especially in the eucharistic species.*

By his power he is present in the sacraments so that when anybody baptises it is really Christ himself who baptises. He is present in his word since it is he himself who speaks when the holy scriptures are read in the Church. Lastly, he is present when the Church prays and sings, for he has promised 'where two or three are gathered together in my name there I am in the midst of them' (Mt 18:20).

Christ, indeed, always associates the Church with himself in this great work in which God is perfectly glorified and men are sanctified. The Church is his beloved Bride who calls to her Lord, and through him offers worship to the eternal Father.

The liturgy, then, is rightly seen as an exercise of the priestly office of Jesus Christ. It involves the presentation of man's sanctification under the guise of signs perceptible by the senses and its accomplishment in ways appropriate to each of these signs. In it full public worship is performed by the Mystical Body of Jesus Christ, that is, by the Head and his members.

From this it follows that every liturgical celebration, because it is an action of Christ the Priest and of his body, which is the Church, is a sacred action surpassing all others. No other action of the Church can equal its efficacy by the same title and to the same degree.

In the earthly liturgy we take part in a foretaste of that heavenly liturgy which is celebrated in the Holy City of Jerusalem toward which we journey as pilgrims, where Christ is sitting at the right hand of God, Minister of the holies and of the true tabernacle. With all the warriors of the heavenly army we sing a hymn of glory to the Lord; venerating the memory of the saints, we hope for some part and fellowship with them; we eagerly await the Saviour, Our Lord Jesus Christ, until he our life shall appear and we too will appear with him in glory.

2

THE CHURCH LISTENING

(Psalm 119)
Blessed are those whose way is
blameless,
who walk in the law of the Lord!
Blessed are those who keep his
testimonies,
who seek him with their whole heart,
who also do no wrong,
but walk in his ways!
Thou hast commanded thy precepts
to be kept diligently.
O that my ways may be steadfast
in keeping thy statutes!
Then I shall not be put to shame,
having my eyes fixed on all thy
commandments.
I will praise thee with an upright heart,
when I learn thy righteous
ordinances.
I will observe thy statutes;
O forsake me not utterly.

How can a young man keep his way
pure?
By guarding it according to thy
word.
With my whole heart I seek thee;
let me not wander from thy
commandments!
I have laid up thy word in my heart,
that I might not sin against thee.

Blessed be thou, O Lord;
  teach me thy statutes!
With my lips I declare
  all the ordinances of thy mouth.
In the way of thy testimonies I delight
  as much as in all riches.
I will meditate on thy precepts,
  and fix my eyes on thy ways.
I will delight in thy statutes;
  I will not forget thy word.

Deal bountifully with thy servant,
  that I may live and observe thy
    word.
Open my eyes, that I may behold
  wondrous things out of thy law.
I am a sojourner on earth;
  hide not thy commandments from
    me!
My soul is consumed with longing
  for thy ordinances at all times.
Thou dost rebuke the insolent, accursed
    ones,
  who wander from thy
    commandments;
take away from me their scorn and
    contempt,
  for I have kept thy testimonies.
Even though princes sit plotting against
    me,
  thy servant will meditate on thy
    statutes.
Thy testimonies are my delight,
  they are my counsellors.

My soul cleaves to the dust;
  revive me according to thy word.
When I told of my ways, thou didst
    answer me;
  teach me thy statutes!
Make me understand the way of thy
    precepts,
  and I will meditate on thy wondrous
    works.
My soul melts away for sorrow;
  strengthen me according to thy word!
Put false ways far from me;
  and graciously teach me thy law.

I have chosen the way of faithfulness,
  I set thy ordinances before me.
I cleave to thy testimonies, O Lord;
  let me not be put to shame!
I will run in the way of thy
    commandments
  when thou enlargest my
      understanding!

Teach me, O Lord, the way of thy
    statutes;
  and I will keep it to the end.
Give me understanding, that I may keep
    thy law
  and observe it with my whole heart.
Lead me in the path of thy
    commandments,
  for I delight in it.
Incline my heart to thy testimonies
  and not to gain!
Turn my eyes from looking at vanities;
  and give me life in thy ways.
Confirm to thy servant thy promise
  which is for those who fear thee.
Turn away the reproach which I dread;
  for thy ordinances are good.
Behold, I long for thy precepts;
  in thy righteousness give me life!

Let thy steadfast love come to me, O
    Lord,
  thy salvation according to thy
      promise;
then shall I have an answer for those
    who taunt me,
  for I trust in thy word.
And take not the word of truth utterly
    out of my mouth,
  for my hope is in thy ordinances.
I will keep thy law continually,
  for ever and ever;
and I shall walk at liberty,
  for I have sought thy precepts.
I will also speak of thy testimonies
    before kings,
  and shall not be put to shame;
for I find my delight in thy
    commandments,
  which I love.

I reverve thy commandments, which I
    love,
    and I will meditate on thy statutes.

Remember thy word to thy servant,
    in which thou hast made me hope.
This is my comfort in my affliction
    that thy promise gives me life.
Godless men utterly deride me,
    but I do not turn away from thy
        law.
When I think of thy ordinances from of
    old,
    I take comfort, O Lord.
Hot indignation seizes me because of the
    wicked
    who forsake thy law.
Thy statutes have been my songs
    in the house of my pilgrimage.
I remember thy name in the night, O
    Lord,
    and keep thy law.
This blessing has fallen to me,
    that I have kept thy precepts.

The Lord is my portion;
    I promise to keep thy words,
I entreat thy favour with all my heart;
    be gracious to me according to thy
        promise
When I think of thy ways,
    I turn my feet to thy testimonies;
I hasten and do not delay
    to keep thy commandments.
Though the cords of the wicked ensnare
    me,
    I do not forget thy law.
At midnight I rise to praise thee,
    because of thy righteous ordinances.
I am a companion of all who fear thee,
    of those who keep thy precepts.
The earth, O Lord, is full of thy
    steadfast love;
    teach me thy statutes!

Thou hast dealt well with thy servant,
    O Lord, according to thy word.
Teach me good judgement and
    knowledge,

for I believe in thy commandments.
Before I was afflicted I went astray;
 but now I keep thy word.
Thou art good and doest good;
 teach me thy statutes.
The godless besmear me with lies,
 but with my whole heart I keep thy
  precepts;
their heart is gross like fat,
 but I delight in thy law.
It is good for me that I was afflicted,
 that I might learn thy statutes.
The law of thy mouth is better to me
 than thousands of gold and silver
  pieces.

Thy hands have made and fashioned
  me;
 give me understanding that I may
  learn thy commandments.
Those who fear thee shall see me and
  rejoice,
 because I have hoped in thy word.
I know, O Lord, that thy judgements
  are right,
 and that in faithfulness thou hast
  afflicted me.
Let thy steadfast love be ready to comfort
  me
 according to thy promise to thy
  servant.
Let thy mercy come to me, that I may
  live;
 for thy law is my delight.
Let the godless be put to shame, because
  they have subverted me with guile;
 as for me, I will meditate on thy
  precepts.
Let those who fear thee turn to me,
 that they may know thy testimonies.
May my heart be blameless in thy
  statutes,
 that I may not be put to shame!

My soul languishes for thy salvation;
 I hope in thy word.
My eyes fail with watching for thy
  promise;

I ask, 'When wilt thou comfort
    me?'
For I have become like a wineskin in
    the smoke,
    yet I have not forgotten thy statutes.
How long must thy servant endure?
    When wilt thou judge those who
        persecute me?
Godless men have dug pitfalls for me,
    men who do not conform to thy law.
All thy commandments are sure;
    they persecute me with falsehood;
        help me!
They have almost made an end of me on
    earth;
    but I have not forsaken thy precepts.
In thy steadfast love spare my life,
    that I may keep the testimonies of
        thy mouth.

For ever, O Lord, thy word
    is firmly fixed in the heavens.
Thy faithfulness endures to all
    generations;
    thou hast established the earth, and
        it stands fast.
By thy appointment they stand this day;
    for all things are thy servants.
If thy law had not been my delight,
    I should have perished in my
        affliction.
I will never forget thy precepts;
    for by them thou hast given me life.
I am thine, save me;
    for I have sought thy precepts.
The wicked lie in wait to destroy me;
    but I consider thy testimonies.
I have seen a limit to all perfection,
    but thy commandment is exceedingly
        broad.

Oh, how I love thy law!
    It is my meditation all the day.
Thy commandment makes me wiser than
    my enemies,
    for it is ever with me.
I have more understanding than all my
    teachers.

for thy testimonies are my
  meditation.
I understand more than the aged,
  for I keep thy precepts.
I hold back my feet from every evil way,
  in order to keep thy word.
I do not turn aside from thy ordinances,
  for thou has taught me.

How sweet are thy words to my taste,
  sweeter than honey to my mouth.
Through thy precepts I get
  understanding;
  therefore I hate every false way.

Thy word is a lamp to my feet
  and a light to my path.
I have sworn an oath and confirm it,
  to observe thy righteous ordinances.
I am sorely afflicted;
  give me life, O Lord, according to
    thy word!
Accept my offerings of praise, O Lord,
  and teach me thy ordinances.
I hold my life in my hand continually,
  but I do not forget thy law.
The wicked have laid a snare for me,
  but I do not stray from thy precepts.
Thy testimonies are my heritage for ever;
  yea, they are the joy of my heart.
I incline my heart to perform thy
    statutes
  for ever, to the end.

I hate double-minded men,
  but I love thy law.
Thou art my hiding place and my
    shield;
  I hope in thy word.
Depart from me, you evildoers,
  that I may keep the commandments
    of my God.
Uphold me according to thy promise,
  that I may live,
  and let me not be put to shame in
    my hope!
Hold me up, that I may be safe
  and have regard for thy statute
    continually!

Thou dost spurn all who go astray from
      thy statutes;
   yea, their cunning is in vain.
All the wicked of the earth thou dost
      count as dross;
   therefore I love thy testimonies.
My flesh trembles for fear of thee
   and I am afraid of thy judgment.

I have done what is just and right,
   do not leave me to my oppressors.
Be surety for thy servant for good;
   let not the godless oppress me.
My eyes fail with watching for thy
      salvation,
      and for the fulfilment of thy
         righteous promise.
Deal with thy servant according to thy
      steadfast love,
   and teach me thy statutes.
I am thy servant; give me
      understanding,
   that I may know thy testimonies!
It is time for the Lord to act,
   for thy law has been broken.
Therefore I love thy commandments
   above gold, above fine gold.
Therefore I direct my steps by all thy
      precepts;
   I hate every false way.

Thy testimonies are wonderful;
   therefore my soul keeps them.
The unfolding of thy words gives light;
   it imparts understanding to the
         simple.
With open mouth I pant,
   because I long for thy
         commandments.
Turn to me and be gracious to me,
   as is thy wont toward those who love
         thy name.
Keep steady my steps according to thy
      promise.
   and let no iniquity get dominion over
         me.
Redeem me from man's oppression,
   that I may keep thy precepts.

Make thy face shine upon thy servant,
and teach me thy statutes.
My eyes shed streams of tears,
because men do not keep thy law.

Righteous art thou, O Lord,
and right are thy judgements.
Thou hast appointed thy testimonies in
righteousness
and in all faithfulness.
My zeal consumes me,
because my foes forget thy words.
Thy promise is well tried,
and thy servant loves it.
I am small and despised,
yet I do not forget thy precepts.
Thy righteousness is righteous for ever,
and thy law is true.
Trouble and anguish have come upon
me,
but thy commandments are my
delight.
Thy testimonies are righteous for ever;
give me understanding that I may
live.

With my whole heart I cry; answer me,
O Lord!
I will keep thy statutes.
I cry to thee; save me,
that I may observe thy testimonies.
I rise before dawn and cry for help;
I hope in thy words.
My eyes are awake before the watches of
the night,
that I may meditate upon thy
promise.
Hear my voice in thy steadfast love;
O Lord, in thy justice preserve my
life.
They draw near who persecute me with
evil purpose;
they are far from thy law.
But thou art near, O Lord,
and all thy commandments are true.
Long have I known from thy testimonies
that thou hast founded them for ever.

Look on my affliction and deliver me,
for I do not forget thy law.
Plead my cause and redeem me;
give me life according to thy promise!
Salvation is far from the wicked,
for they do not seek thy statutes.
Great is thy mercy, O Lord;
give me life according to thy justice.
Many are my persecutors and my
adversaries,
but I do not swerve from thy
testimonies.
I look at the faithless with disgust,
because they do not keep thy
commands.
Consider how I love thy precepts!
Preserve my life according to thy
steadfast love.
The sum of thy word is truth;
and every one of thy righteous
ordinances endures for ever.

Princes persecute me without cause,
but my heart stands in awe of thy
words.
I rejoice at thy word
like one who finds great spoil.
I hate and abhor falsehood,
but I love thy law.
Seven times a day I praise thee
for thy righteous ordinances.
Great peace have those who love thy
law;
nothing can make them stumble.
I hope for thy salvation, O Lord,
and I do thy commandments.
My soul keeps thy testimonies;
I love them exceedingly.
I keep thy precepts and testimonies,
for all my ways are before thee.

Let my cry come before thee, O Lord;
give me understanding according to
thy word!
Let my supplication come before thee;
deliver me according to thy word.
My lips will pour forth praise
that thou dost teach me thy statutes.

My tongue will sing of thy word,
    for all thy commandments are right.
Let thy hand be ready to help me,
    for I have chosen thy precepts.
I long for thy salvation, O Lord,
    and thy law is my delight.
Let me live, that I may praise thee,
    and let thy ordinances help me.
I have gone astray like a lost sheep; seek
        thy servant,
    for I do not forget thy
        commandments.

From the Acts of the Apostles *(6:1-4.7)*

Now in these days when the disciples were increasing in number, the Hellenists murmured against the Hebrews because their widows were neglected in the daily distribution. And the twelve summoned the body of the disciples and said 'It is not right that we should give up preaching the word of God to serve tables. Therefore, brethren, pick out from among you seven men of good repute, full of the Spirit and of wisdom, whom we may appoint to this duty. But we will devote ourselves to prayer and to the ministry of the word. ... And the word of God increased; and the number of the disciples multiplied greatly in Jerusalem, and a great many of the priests were obedient to the faith.

From the Letter to the Hebrews *(4:12-13)*

For the word of God is living and active, sharper than any two-edged sword, piercing to the division of soul and spirit, of joints and marrow, and discerning the thoughts and intentions of the heart. And before him no creature is hidden, but all are open and laid bare to the eyes of him with whom we have to do.

From *Dei Verbum*, nn. *21-25 (passim)*

21.   *The Church has always venerated the divine scriptures as she venerated the body of the Lord, in so far as she never ceases, particularly in the sacred liturgy, to partake of the bread of life and to offer it to the faithful from the one table of the Word of God and the Body of Christ. She has always regarded, and continues to regard the Scriptures, taken together with sacred tradition, as the supreme rule of her faith. For, since they are inspired by God and committed to writing once and for all time, they present God's own Word in an unalterable form, and they make the voice of the Holy*

Spirit sound again and again in the words of the prophets and apostles. It follows that all the preaching of the Church, as indeed the entire Christian religion should be nourished and ruled by sacred Scripture. In the sacred books the Father who is in heaven comes lovingly to meet his children, and talks with them. And such is the force and power of the Word of God that it can serve the Church as her support and vigour, and the children of the Church as strength for their faith, food for the soul, and a pure and lasting fount of spiritual life.

22. *Access to sacred scripture ought to be open wide to the Christian faithful ....*

25. *Likewise, the sacred Synod forcefully and specifically exhorts all the Christian faithful, especially those who live the religious life, to learn 'the surpassing knowledge of Jesus Christ' (Phil. 3:8) by frequent reading of the divine Scriptures. 'Ignorance of the Scriptures is ignorance of Christ' (St Jerome). Therefore, let them go gladly to the sacred text itself, whether in the sacred liturgy, which is full of the divine words, or in devout reading, or in such suitable exercises and various other helps which, with the approval and guidance of the pastors of the Church, are happily spreading everywhere in our way.*

Let them remember, however, that prayer should accompany the reading of sacred scripture, so that a dialogue takes place between God and man. For 'we speak to him when we pray; we listen to him when we read the divine oracles' (St Ambrose).

Introductory psalm
In our programme of reflections on the Second Vatican Council today, we shall concentrate this evening on the Dogmatic Constitution on Divine Revelation (*Dei Verbum* — DV) which presents the Church as listening to the Word. The constitution is very helpful in deepening the image of the Church which we are called upon to live in our communities.

As a preparation I would invite you to recite Psalm 119 — a very long and rather special type of psalm. It has in all 176 verses, divided into 22 stanzas, each having eight verses. Each of the 22 stanzas begins with a letter of the Hebrew alphabet and in each of the eight verses there is a synonym for 'the law'. Thus we find the terms *precept, justice, decree, judgment, commandment, teaching, statutes, laws* ...

In what is admittedly a pretty artificial construction, the psalmist indicates that the law of God is all-embracing, teaches us everything, is a guide for each person throughout the entire day. There is a tremendous sense of fulfilment and love in this psalm; it is like a melody whose invocations, ejaculations and acts of adoration gather us up together and dispose us to open our hearts to the Word of God.

While reciting the psalm we should be mindful that the law, the precepts and the teachings are in fact Jesus Christ. He is the ultimate truth of the psalm, the definitive Word who reveals the fullness of God's plan for humanity.

I would suggest that you give particular emphasis to those verses where 'the Word of God' is expressly mentioned. One of the most beautiful verses — in my view among the most beautiful in the Bible — is the one which says: 'Thy word is a lamp to my feet and a light to my path'. (v 105) And again, 'Deal bountifully with thy servant, that I may live and observe thy word' (17).

The Dogmatic Constitution *Dei Verbum*

If I were to ask you what *Dei Verbum* talks about I am sure that many of you would immediately answer 'the word of God'. Others may well say that it speaks especially about the Scriptures, of the books of the Bible. When we read the document attentively we discover that from chapter III onwards it speaks *only* of the Scriptures. In fact, chapter III deals with the inspiration and interpretation of the sacred books; chapter IV deals with the Old Testament, chapter V with the New Testament and chapter VI with Scriptures in the life of the Church. Thus, about three-quarters of the document deals with scripture. Its proper title is, in fact, *Dogmatic Constitution on Divine Revelation*.

It is therefore necessary to grasp the relationship between revelation and scripture and between scripture and Word. We frequently use these terms as if they were synonymous and it is true that their meanings are closely interrelated. However, as the Council document suggests, we need to be more precise.

In the *Prologue* the intention of the Council Fathers is expressed in the following terms:

> Hearing the Word of God with reverence .... following in
> the steps of the Councils of Trent and Vatican I, this Synod

wishes to set forth the true doctrine on divine revelation and its transmission.

What then is the importance of what is said in the *Prologue* in relation to scripture and the Word of God? The document responds by pointing out the relationship between revelation, Word of God, transmission of revelation and scripture, thus giving us a clear idea of the complexity of these concepts which are fundamental to the Christian life and to the pastoral work of our parishes. We will try, rather hurriedly, to present the exposition of the Council.

Revelation and the Word of God

The Council's starting point is divine initiative. 'It pleased God to reveal himself.' It pleased God to make himself known, to manifest himself, to communicate himself, to make known his loving plan. This is the source and origin of all reality: the divine loving salvific will of God who wishes to communicate with us, make himself known to us.

In this *revelation* 'the invisible God from the fullness of his love speaks to humanity' (DV 2). By the expression *Word of God* we mean his act of self-revelation.

But the act of a person, of an intelligent being who addresses other intelligent beings, is expressed in words, conversation, verbal communication and other elements having a certain analogy with verbal communication.

The Word of God means God's self-communication to humanity. But there is more. God's conversation with humanity 'is realised by *deeds* and *words*' (DV 2). The *deeds* are the loving acts which go from the exodus of the people of Israel to the death of Jesus on the cross; acts which go from creation to the call of Abraham to the call of Paul. Deeds are steeped in words, words are joined to deeds: all together they make up an activity which is communication and divine revelation. This is how God speaks.

His self-revelation in deeds and words culminates in Christ, the Word *par excellence,* the definitive Word which reveals God to humanity and in which humanity knows the mystery of God; Christ the Word of the Father.

Hence the expression, *primacy of the Word* is justified. But though I use it often myself, I have sometimes asked myself, what does primacy of the Word mean? Is it not the sort of expression that belongs rather to other Christian denominations?

The primacy of the Word is the quintessence of Revelation; it is the primacy of God in his activity of self-revelation, self-communication, self-manifestation! I referred to this in my second pastoral letter — *In the beginning the Word*. What is at stake is the foundational nature of the Word, its primordial importance as source and origin of all.

If the world exists, if we exist, if we have a meaning and a hope it is because God speaks and communicates himself. The Word is a living person, not a formal abstract reality.

The Word is above all Christ, the full revelation of the Father, and then it is the entire plan of mediation which God has used and continues to use to transmit his message, to reveal himself to humanity and to reveal our real identity to us, inviting us, pressing us to live up to the responsibilities of our vocation. Such is the Word of God.

Word of God, faith and charity

The Word of God, his act of self-communication, of communicating through deeds and words is mediated by sacred writers, by prophets, the apostles, the utterances of Jesus himself, all coming together in the sacred Scriptures which record, report and contain this Word of God. The text from Hebrews, which we read, describes the power of the Word. In chapter 4 the author explains Psalm 95 which speaks of the repose which God will grant to his people; he applies it to the current situation of believers and then concludes: 'For the Word of God is living and active, sharper than any two-edged sword, piercing to the division of the soul and spirit, of joints and marrow and discerning the thoughts and intentions of the heart' *(Heb 4:12)*. Such is the power of the Word of God and of the Word of God contained in the scriptures: it is not a dead word, as in human books; it is not merely a record of the past. The Word has power for *today*, because it carries within itself the same power with which God pronounced it and continues to pronounce it in history.

1. Where does the power of the Word of God principally lie? *In arousing faith*. What corresponds in us to the Word of God

is faith. The Word is on God's side: he shares, reveals himself, gives himself, invites, promises, judges, commands and exhorts. On our side there is faith, the response which we give to God: we hear, receive, welcome, obey, allow ourselves to be enlightened, encouraged, consoled, comforted, inspired by the Word through which God communicates his mystery of love and calls on us to become his children, to share in his mystery forever. Faith, therefore, corresponds to the primacy of the Word.

If the Word does not meet with the response of faith, it resounds in the air; it lacks effectiveness. When the Word is, on the other hand, received by us in an attitude of faith, it exerts all its effectiveness.

2.   The *effectiveness* which the Word heard in faith exerts in *charity*. The seed is the Word: faith is the womb, the ground which welcomes the seed; charity is the fruit which is born of that seed.

From this very simple structure of the process of salvation we can draw extremely important conclusions for our pastoral work. Do we want to grow in charity? Let us strengthen the roots of our faith by *opening ourselves to hear the Word.* It would be pointless to pretend that there could be greater charity in the community without growth in faith.

It would be equally vain to pretend that there is a growth in faith if there is not a deeper listening to the Word. The process — Word, faith, charity — constitutes the living reality on which all pastoral work is based.

Unfortunately, this process is frequently ignored or bypassed, almost as if we could short-circuit the process and bring about charity by simple exhortations that are not rooted in faith. We act as if we could bring about a growth and strengthening of faith in people without pouring into them the abundant treasures of the Word of God.

You who are directly involved in the work of parishes are called to deepen in yourselves this fundamental teaching of the Council: we begin with the Word; faith is the response; charity the fruit.

We found further proof for this pastoral plan in our reading from chapter 6 of the Acts of the apostles. The problem there was the establishment of priorities. A certain number of injustices arose from the manner in which goods were shared. So, we might say, let us organise our charity better. Precisely because the

36

organisation of charity was not working well, the Apostles decided to devote themselves to the Word and to prayer — delegating to others the area of charitable activity. They are aware that at the root of everything, the principle from which all action flows is the Word, with prayer as a response in faith. Without this root there cannot be the fruit of charity.

The people of God have a right to demand that their Bishops and pastors are above all men of the Word and of prayer so that they can then be instigators of charity.

Charity and an adequate response to needs are urgent priorities for the Church. Yet each one of us, precisely because of this urgency, should remain convinced of the priority, of the primary necessity of the Word: listening to the Word is the first and most urgent task of the Church of God.

Scripture and the Word of God

In listening to the Word, Scripture has a fundamental role to play. The Scriptures are the record of God's revealing deeds and words. They are a record written under divine initiative, authority and responsibility; they have a divine guarantee, through the inspiration received by the inspired authors, the human instruments of their composition.

The Bible is not merely the authentic record of the Word: more accurately it contains the Word; it is itself the Word being revealed, it is revelation in action through the power of the Spirit who inspired it and causes it to be proclaimed in the Church.

Naturally, scripture should not be considered as something bookish, as if the words deprived of any context had some sort of magical power! Scripture has to be profoundly integrated with Revelation, with faith and with grace and the Holy Spirit. Only in this context can scripture be considered as a *revealing Word for today*; only in this context is it active and effective, reaching the hearts of all who listen to it, enlivening faith and bearing fruits of charity.

Hence we can see the incomparable dignity of scripture, which has rightly been likened to the Body of Christ: 'The Church has always venerated the divine Scriptures as she venerated the Body of the Lord' (DV 21).

Let me repeat: the Bible not only contains but *is* the Word of God, that rings out in the Church and through history; it nourishes the believer, who listens to it in humility and obedience; it encourages, consoles, comforts and illuminates just as the sacramental Body of Christ nourishes, encourages, consoles and comforts.

The Word of the Scriptures in fact is inseparable from the historical body of Christ: Where, if not in the Gospels, do we learn what Jesus did during the period of his earthly existence? The Eucharistic body of Christ which is made present in our altars is inseparable from the Scriptures: the Eucharist is effected through words which are found in the Scriptures; it is explained during the liturgy, again with words from the Scriptures; it is situated in the saving plan as revealed and described in the Scriptures.

Scriptures, the historical Christ, the Eucharistic Christ — these are three strictly related realities and it would be heresy to separate them or to claim to understand them in isolation. Rather we should constantly strive to place them in the living context in which the Word of God still resounds today, as in the time of Abraham, Moses or Jesus, through the power of the same Holy Spirit in the Church of God.

General conclusions and practical questions
1.   Our *first* conclusion is obvious. We ought to *venerate* the sacred Scriptures as we venerate the Body of the Lord, thanking God for the gift of the Scriptures.

The *second* is that we ought to *approach* the Scriptures. A long time before the Council Paul Claudel remarked that Christians proved their great veneration for the Scriptures by keeping well away from them!

Real veneration means that we approach the Scriptures: we should read them, own a Bible, and not be afraid to underline passages.

The *third* conclusion is that we ought to *meditate* on the Scriptures. We ought to practise the *lectio divina* about which I have spoken so often. This means that we should read the Word of God *as* the Word of God. 'This Sacred Synod, ardently and with insistence exhorts all the faithful to learn the "surpassing worth of knowing Christ Jesus" *(Phil. 3:8)* through frequent reading of the divine Scriptures' (DV 25). It is a very strong exhortation addressed to us by the Council and we are only too aware of not meeting its demands.

2. Following on these conclusions, I would like to pose a number of questions:

— Do I own a copy of the Scriptures? More than likely you will have a copy somewhere at home, but what I am asking is, do you have it to hand, do you use it?

— Do I know the Scriptures? Do I know what the words of scripture mean for my life? What influence do the words of the Gospels in particular have on my life? Putting the question the other way round: What kind of person would I be without the words of the Gospel in my life? Can I discover choices, attitudes, decisions or desires where the Gospel has been or continues to be a determining factor? What passages from the Gospel most influence my life? This may well prove to be a very fruitful self-examination. We may well find that the Gospel is more a part of our make-up than we had imagined.

— Do I meditate on the Scriptures? All of us and especially those more intimately involved in parish councils, should meditate on the Scriptures for at least ten minutes every day. This would be a very practical way of responding to the Council's exhortation. The Council in fact goes beyond merely suggesting: it asks us to read the Scriptures frequently and prayerfully, beginning with the Gospels, then the Acts of the Apostles, the Letters of Paul and the Psalms, then going back to the prophets, to the Exodus and the Book of Genesis.

There are many useful publications available nowadays which indicate an order and methods of approaching the Bible.

Before concluding I would like to read two passages from a Father of the Church who is very dear to me — St Gregory the Great — in whose writings, as you know, I found my episcopal motto.

In the first passage he speaks of an experience which I must say has frequently been my own — reading the Scriptures with the faithful in order to get a better understanding of them. In the bosom of the Christian community, aspects that in private reading remained unclear are revealed. 'I know from experience that frequently in the company of my brothers I have understood

39

many things about the Word of God that on my own I did not succeed in understanding. It is you who enable me to learn what I teach. This is the truth: rather often I tell you that which I hear when I am with you' (*In Ezech* 2.2.1). Hence the importance for members of parish councils of reading the Scriptures *together*.

The second passage is contained in a letter which Gregory sent to a dear friend, the Emperor's physician, in June 595. He begins with friendly greetings and then goes on to reprove his friend: 'I give thanks to God that spiritual union is not broken by physical distance. We are, my dear friend, bodily at a distance from each other but spiritually we are united in charity ... Since it is true that the more you love someone the more outspoken you can be, let me tell you that I have to reprimand you, dear illustrious Theodorus. The Holy Trinity has bestowed on you gifts of understanding, of goods, as well as mercy and charity. In spite of this you allow yourself to be overcome by secular cares, with continuous comings and goings, so that you neglect your daily reading of the words of your Redeemer.' (You will note that St Gregory is not writing to a monk but to a very busy and committed lay person and yet he reprimands him for not reading the Scriptures *daily*.)

'What is sacred scripture if not a letter from God to his creature? If you were to find yourself away from headquarters, posted in some distant place and you received a letter from your earthly emperor you would not be at ease, you would not go to rest or have a nap until you found out what your emperor had to say to you. The emperor of the heavens, the Lord of the Angels and of humankind has sent you his letters. They have a bearing on your very life and yet, my son, you show no anxiety to read these letters! Get down to it, I implore you, and find a way to meditate *daily* on the words of your creator. Learn to know the mind of God in the Word of God' (from the letter to Theodorus, personal physician to the Emperor).

During our adoration of the Eucharist let this be the grace which we ask for each other; 'Grant O Lord, that we may discover your mind in your words'.

3

THE CHURCH AS MYSTERY AND COMMUNION

(Psalm 122)
I was glad when they said to me,
'Let us go to the house of the Lord!'
Our feet have been standing
within your gates, O Jerusalem!

Jerusalem, built as a city
which is bound firmly together,
to which the tribes go up,
the tribes of the Lord,
as was decreed for Israel,
to give thanks to the name of the Lord.
There thrones for judgment were set,
the thrones of the house of David.

Pray for the peace of Jerusalem!
'May they prosper who love you!
Peace be within your walls,
and security within your towers!'

For my brethren and companions' sake
I will say, 'peace be within you!'
For the sake of the house of the
Lord our God
I will seek your good.

From the Letter to the Ephesians *(4:1-16)*
I therefore, a prisoner for the Lord, beg you to lead a life worthy of the
calling to which you have been called, with all lowliness and meekness,

41

with patience, forbearing one another in love, eager to maintain the unity of the Spirit in the bond of peace. There is one body and one Spirit, just as you were called to the one hope that belongs to your call, one Lord, one faith, one baptism, one God and Father of us all, who is above all and through all and in all. But grace was given to each of us according to the measure of Christ's gift. Therefore it is said:

'When he ascended on high he led a host of captives, and he gave gifts to men'. (In saying, 'he ascended' what does it mean but that he had also descended into the lower parts of the earth? He who descended is he who also ascended far above all the heavens, that he might fill all things). And his gifts were that some should be apostles, some prophets, some evangelists, some pastors and teachers for the equipment of the saints, for the work of ministry, for building up the body of Christ until we all attain to the unity of the faith and of the knowledge of the Son of God, to mature manhood, to the measure of the stature of the fullness of Christ; so that we may no longer be children, tossed to and fro and carried about with every wind of doctrine, by the cunning of men, by their craftiness in deceitful wiles. Rather speaking the truth in love, we are to grow up in every way into him who is the head, into Christ, from whom the whole body, joined and knit together by every joint with which it is supplied, when each part is working properly, makes bodily growth and upbuilds itself in love.

From the Acts of the Apostles *(4:31-35)*
And when they had prayed, the place in which they were gathered together was shaken; and they were all filled with the Holy Spirit and spoke the word of God with boldness. Now the company of those who believed were of one heart and soul, and no one said that any of the things which he possessed was his own, but they had everything in common. And with great power the apostles gave their testimony to the resurrection of the Lord Jesus, and great grace was upon them all. There was not a needy person among them, for as many as were possessors of lands or houses sold them, and brought the proceeds of what was sold and laid it at the apostles' feet; and distribution was made to each as any had need.

From the Dogmatic Constitution on the Church *Lumen gentium* *(n.8)*
The one mediator, Christ, established and ever sustains here on earth his holy Church, the community of faith, hope and charity, as a visible organisation through which he communicates truth and grace to all men. But, the society structured with hierarchical organs and the mystical body

of Christ, the visible society and the spiritual community, the earthly Church and the Church endowed with heavenly riches, are not to be thought of as two realities. On the contrary, they form one complex reality which comes together from a human and a divine element. For this reason the Church is compared, not without significance, with the mystery of the incarnate Word. As the assumed nature, inseparably united to him, serves the divine Word as a living organ of salvation, so, in a somewhat similar way, does the social structure of the Church serve the Spirit of Christ who vivifies it, in the building up of the body. (cf. Eph 4:15).

This is the sole Church of Christ which in the Creed we profess to be one, holy, catholic and apostolic, which our Saviour, after his resurrection, entrusted to Peter's pastoral care (cf Jn 21:17), *commissioning him and the other apostles to extend and rule it* (cf. Matt. 28:18, etc.), *and which he raised up for all ages as 'the pillar and mainstay of the truth'* (I Tim 3:15).

This Church constituted and organised as a society in the present world, subsists in the Catholic Church, which is governed by the successor of Peter and by the bishops in communion with him. Nevertheless, many elements of sanctification and of truth are found outside its visible confines. Since these are gifts belonging to the Church of Christ, they are forces impelling towards Catholic unity.

Introductory psalm

'Grant us O Lord so to reflect on the mystery of the Church that we may be enabled to assume the ecclesial responsibility proper to each one of us in our own local communities. Grant too that we may contemplate this mystery of which we ourselves are a part and of which we are called on to be builders'.

Psalm 122 is the starting point for this evening's reflection. Many among us have recited it on the way to the Holy City. The psalm describes an aspect of the Church using the image of Jerusalem. It begins with the words 'I was glad when they said to me, "Let us go to the house of the Lord" '. It is, after all, the psalm used by pilgrims on their ascent to the *temple*. Immediately the vista is enlarged to take in the entire city 'Our feet have been standing within our gates, O Jerusalem', which is now contemplated in its unity. Various aspects of the city are lovingly admired: the gates, the robust construction of the walls, the compact array of houses. In the context of this robust strength, the unity of mind, or communion, is underlined: 'to which the tribes go up *together*'.

Together is the key word in the Acts of the Apostles, in the life of the Church of the New Testament. They go up together according to the law of Israel *'to give thanks to the name of the Lord'*. In Jerusalem too are to be found 'the thrones of judgement'. In their coming together therefore they contemplate the realities that go to make up the internal cohesion of the Church: law, praise, prayer, liturgy and judgment. These are the realities that made of the Church a juridical community and a community of praise in which peace flourishes. We should note in the psalm the triple mention of peace — 'Pray for peace ... peace (prosperity) to those who love you ... peace be within your walls ...'

Peace, which then becomes security, is the final invocation of the psalmist: 'I will say "peace be within you".'

Let us ask for a profound understanding of this firm, compact Church in which *together* we give praise to God and we live in peace and brotherhood: Let us ask for the gift of being able to contemplate it, the ability to open our eyes to the marvels of the Church and the grace to thank God, One and Three, daily for the Church.

Eight beatitudes of the Church

Would it not be wonderful if at the end of our prayers this evening this very cathedral were to tremble just as when the early Christians were gathered for prayer — 'And when they had prayed, the place in which they were gathered together was shaken; and they were all filled with the Holy Spirit and spoke the word of God with boldness' *(Acts 4:31)*. Would it not be splendid if we were all filled with the Holy Spirit and eager to proclaim the word of God with boldness?

Let us hope that this will be the fruit of our meditation. We will be meditating on the very core and centre of the mystery of God, the Church as mystery and communion. We will draw our inspiration from the Dogmatic Constitution *Lumen gentium* — probably the finest of the documents of Vatican II and the one which during the years the Council met was worked through with the greatest passion and intensity. You may also know that, together with the document *Gaudium et spes* it was the Constitution most quoted during the most recent Extraordinary Synod of Bishops.

Lumen gentium is composed of eight short chapters and I remember with admiration a group of young people whom I met, who had used the document in preparing for Confirmation: they could almost recite it from memory! I could summarise the eight chapters in the form of eight beatitudes of the Church:

Blessed is the Church for she is mystery;
Blessed is the Church for she is the people of God!
Blessed is the Church for her hierarchy.
Blessed is the Church for her laity!
Blessed is the Church for her religious men and women!
Blessed is the Church for her eternal destiny!
Blessed is the Church for her mother Mary!

The Church as mystery

I will not attempt to comment on all the eight beatitudes as presented in the Council document. I will confine myself to the first as it is the root of all the others. 'Blessed is the Church *for she is mystery!* and I would add — *'for she is a communion'*. Let us begin by examining the notion of mystery.

The word *mystery* seems immediately to evoke the idea of something obscure or hidden, of being inaccessible to reason. On the other hand it is used very frequently in *Lumen gentium* (at least twenty-three times) (*Sacrament* and *mystery* are very closely connected in the original Latin meaning of the words.). Perhaps the most interesting place to begin our investigation is in the final Report made at the Synod of Bishops where there is great emphasis on *mystery*.

What did the Synod do? It began with an updated understanding of the 'signs of the times' which do not coincide with those of twenty years ago. 'Among these signs of the times special mention must be given to *secularism*. There is no doubt that the Council vindicated the legitimate autonomy of the temporal sphere. This is secularism properly understood. But here we are dealing with a totally different reality. This type of secularism consists of a totally autonomistic view of man and the world which prescinds from the idea of mystery, but rather neglects or denies it. This immanentism diminishes the integral vision of the human person.' It denies mystery and prescinds from it. Hence, what is opposed to this type of secularism, to this kind of closed vision of reality, is mystery. 'However, there are signs today of a new hunger and thirst for the transcendent'. (*Final Report,* part 2, A,1).

It is therefore necessary to rekindle in people's minds and hearts an openness to the divine dimension of things and the dimension of mystery. In this way the Synod went so far as to make central the notion of mystery and its importance for today's world. We must speak of the Church as mystery in order to avoid a reductionist interpretation of its meaning and in order to promote in people an openness to a vision of the transcendent.

Given this premise the members of the Synod dwell at some length on the mystery of God and the mystery of the Church.

'Mystery of God' has a very precise meaning: it is the divine eternal plan for our salvation through Jesus Christ in the Holy Spirit. It is the divine salvific plan unknown to us but revealed in the Gospel through which each one of us is called to salvation in Christ and in the Holy Spirit. This mystery is spelled out in *Lumen gentium* (n.2) just as we have seen it at the beginning of *Dei Verbum:* 'It pleased God, in his goodness and wisdom, to reveal himself and to make known the mystery of his will. His will was that men should have access to the Father, through Christ, the Word made flesh, in the Holy Spirit and thus become sharers in the divine nature' (*Dei Verbum* n.2).

If the mystery of God is his saving plan for us in Christ, then the Church is 'sacrament, sign and instrument' of this mystery. This is her purpose; she gives expression to this plan, she contains it, makes it present, but at the same time she remains totally relative to the mystery. The Church is not, of itself, the first mystery. The first mystery is the salvation of humanity brought about by God in Jesus; it is Jesus himself. The Church is mystery in so far as she is related to Christ; she is the beginning of the fullness of the Kingdom in which the mystery of salvation is achieved. The Church is the reign of Christ present in mystery and the final Report of the Synod makes a strongly worded statement on the essential relationship of the Church to Jesus:

'The Church would become more credible if she spoke less of herself and preached Christ crucified more (see I Cor 2:27). In this way the Church is sacrament. As such she is a sign and an instrument of communion with God and of communion and reconciliation amongst people ... The entire importance of the

46

Church derives from her relationship with Christ ... all that is said about the Church has to be understood in the light of the mystery of Christ or of the Church in Christ. Jesus Christ is always present in his Church, and lives in her as the Risen One'.

From this relationship with Christ are included all the other characteristics of the Church as described by *Lumen gentium* and presented earlier in this chapter as the beatitudes of the Church. (cf. *Final Report*, part 2, A, 2, 3). Thus these eight beatitudes which I enumerated might be completed by a ninth: Blessed is the Church for her poverty, for what she is is a total gift of God and of Christ; blessed is the Church for everything that she has is Christ continuously and mysteriously operating in her.

Thus the Church sees herself mirrored in the Virgin Mary and in her canticle: 'My soul magnifies the Lord, and my spirit rejoices in God my Saviour, for he has regarded the low estate of his handmaid. For behold, henceforth all generations will call me blessed' *(Luke 1:46-48)*.

The Church can be called 'blessed' because nothing that she has is her own, because in her poverty she is loved by God who showers her with gifts: Christ, the first gift, and with all the treasures of wisdom and understanding. And we are this Church.

From the consideration of the Church as mystery follow adoration and praise for what we are as a Church, as a gift of God. This praise is rooted in our poverty.

Some of the Council Fathers were anxious to have a fourth session of Vatican II which would summarise the work of the Council under the theme of the poverty of the Church. I recall a document proposed by Cardinal Giacomo Lercaro which proposed a synthesis of the Council's work centred on the notion of poverty, in a draft which he was able to present to Paul VI.

However, the Vatican Council did not extend over another year, it already had gone on for a long time. And so it falls to us to understand the mystery of the poverty of the Church. This poverty is at the very root of the riches given to her by Christ. From this flows the intimate relationship between the Church and the poor, the Church's preoccupation with the cause of the poor and her presence in the midst of the various manifestations of human poverty. Here too is the origin of all forms of charity of the Church, of a Church at one and the same time poor and infinitely enriched through the mercy of God. From this arises the praise of the Church who wishes to exult in the Eucharist, in thanksgiving for the love God has shown her.

All this is grace; we should receive with joy and welcome with gratitude and, since all that we have is given to us, we too should give freely. This fact is at the heart of our missionary witness. It is the witness that arises from the recognition that what we have is not obvious nor paid for, but is a reality with which God engifts us, day by day, hour by hour. God is continuously giving us his Christ and with him all things and, indeed, making us into his Church.

The Church as communion

The idea of the Church as communion flows directly from our reflection on the Church as mystery.

The extraordinary Synod of Bishops in the second part of the *Final Report,* develops amply the theme of communion and shows that it is derived from the reality of mystery. 'Since the Church is mystery it is the mystery of communion and is a sacrament of communion with God and reconciliation amongst people'. A number of important consequences for the internal life of the Church itself are to be drawn from the notion of Church as Communion: the unity and pluriformity of the Church; the Oriental Churches; collegiality; episcopal conferences; participation and coresponsibility within the Church; ecumenism. 'The ecclesiology of communion,' the *Report* affirms, 'is the basic and central idea in the Council Documents'. (cf. *Final Report,* part 2, C, 1.)

What does it mean to say that the Church is communion? It is important to understand this in order to understand the Church and its nature. 'Basically we are dealing with communion with God, through Jesus Christ, in the Holy Spirit' *(ibid).* The whole point of God's saving plan is the communion of humanity with God, through Jesus in the Holy Spirit.

'And this communion', the *Report* continues, 'takes place in the Word of God and in the sacraments' (as we have already said, *Dei Verbum* and *Sacrosanctum Concilium* are the two Council documents that elaborate these themes). 'Baptism is the door to, and the foundation stone of, this communion. The Eucharist is at one and the same time the source and climax of the whole Christian life. Communion with the Eucharistic Body of Christ signifies and effects, that is, it builds up the intimate communion of all the faithful in the Body of Christ which is the Church' *(ibid)*.

The fact that we are Church is therefore the fruit of the Eucharist; it is not the result of our wishing one another well, or even our coming together to pray. Rather, God himself makes us into a *communion* by nourishing us with his Word and with his Body. He makes us a communion, a closely-knit reality, bound by a relationship that has no parallel in other human relationships. In this fashion communion comes from God to people and reaches humanity through the Church.

Practical conclusions

How are we to grasp in a concrete way the wonderful things that we have been trying to express? In the first instance let us begin by contemplating them in Eucharistic adoration: 'Eucharistic Jesus, you who are the life source of communion, grant that we may understand how communion is the high point and the main aim of the divine plan of salvation and how it makes us Church'. In the second instance let us be guided by the Word of God which was proclaimed.

'I therefore, a prisoner for the Lord, beg you to lead a life worthy of the calling to which you have been called, with all lowliness and meekness, with patience, forbearing one another in love, eager to maintain the unity of the Spirit in the bond of peace' *(Eph 4:1-3)*. 'Now the company of those who believed were of one heart and soul, and no one said that any of the things which he possessed was his own, but they had everything in common. And with great power the Apostles gave their testimony to the resurrection of the Lord Jesus, and great grace was upon them all. There was not a needy person among them, for as many as were possessors of lands or houses sold them, and brought the proceeds of what was sold and laid it at the apostles' feet; and distribution was made to each as any had need' *(Acts 4: 32-35)*.

We can draw three conclusions:
1. We should live *intensely the mystery of the Church* in the universal dimension of the Church (communion with the Pope) and its local dimension, that is the diocese.

Let us ask for the grace to live these realities intensely and to interiorise them in our lives.

2.   We should be *ready to serve*. Our intense living out of the mystery of the Church would be of no avail if we were not willing to do something for the Church, to allow ourselves to be drawn by the divine movement of the Spirit who draws us towards the fullness of Christ.

Each one of us can ask this question: Am I really at the disposal of my Church, my diocese, my parish? In the context of parish councils how do I live out my commitment to be of service?

3.   We should understand *the Church as mystery*, as sacrament and instrument in which God acts really and invisibly. This level of understanding requires that we avoid taking a narrow view, that we shun gossip and slander, as well as mean-minded judgments that risk closing the community or the group or pastoral councils in on themselves.

Every time we lose sight of the grandeur of the mystery by dwelling on the shortcomings of persons, the weakness of the group, the poverty of some current situation in the Church or of some initiative, we risk losing ourselves in minutiae through lack of vision and of ability to reflect on the infinite mystery of God who works through these weak and poor realities. We as a Church are indeed poor but we are rich with the riches of God.

As soon as we broaden our horizons, judgements cease and bickerings fade, our hearts expand. When faith becomes opaque and inflexible, our hearts grow stunted and the Church, like any other society, is weighed down by pettiness and idle gossip. When this happens we see how far we have strayed from our vision of mystery and how are reduced to living the poverty of the Church not as an enriching gift of God, but rather as a sad and miserable undertaking.

'Grant us Lord to remain always mindful of the mysterious nature of the Church and always to see in her your salvific work in action'.

These three conclusions might well become the subject of our examination of conscience before the Eucharist.

— Do I live the life of the local Church with intensity?
— Am I ready to be of service, and in what way?
— Do I understand the Church as mystery in such a way that my judgements, my options, are fired by the enthusiastic love

that is born of contemplating in her the mystery of God and communion with Christ achieved through the grace of the Holy Spirit?

4

THE CHURCH AS A SIGN AND INSTRUMENT OF UNITY

From the Prophet Isaiah *(2:2-5)*
It shall come to pass in the latter days that the mountain of the house of the Lord shall be established as the highest of the mountains, and shall be raised above the hills; and all the nations shall flow to it, and many peoples shall come, and say: 'Come, let us go up to the mountain of the Lord, to the house of the God of Jacob; that he may teach us his ways and that we may walk in his paths.' For out of Zion shall go forth the law, and the word of the Lord from Jerusalem. He shall judge between the nations, and shall decide for many peoples; and they shall beat their swords into ploughshares, and their spears into pruning hooks; nation shall not lift up sword against nation, neither shall they learn war any more. O, House of Jacob, come, let us walk in the light of the Lord.

For the Letter to the Romans *(8:18-27)*
I consider that the sufferings of this present time are not worth comparing with the glory that is to be revealed to us. For the creation waits with eager longing for the revealing of the sons of God; for the creation was subjected to futility, not of its own will but by the will of him who subjected it in hope; because the creation itself will be set free from its bondage to decay and obtain the glorious liberty of the children of God. We know that the whole creation has been groaning in travail together until now; and not only creation, but we ourselves, who have the first fruits of the Spirit, groan inwardly as we wait for adoption as sons, the redemption of our bodies. For in this hope we were saved. Now hope that is seen is not hope. For who hopes for what he sees? But if we hope for what we do not see, we wait for it with patience.

Likewise the Spirit helps us in our weakness; for we do not know how to pray as we ought, but the Spirit himself intercedes for us with sighs too deep for words. And he who searches the hearts of men knows that is the mind of the Spirit, because the Spirit intercedes for the saints according to the will of God.

From the Pastoral Constitution, The Church in the Modern World, *Gaudium et spes,* (nn. 3 and 11)

3. In wonder at their own discoveries and their own might men are today troubled and perplexed by questions about current trends in the world, about their place and their role in the universe, about the meaning of individual and collective endeavour, and finally about the destiny of nature and of men. And so the Council, as witness and guide to the faith of the whole people of God, gathered together by Christ, can find no more eloquent expression of its solidarity and respectful affection for the whole human family, to which it belongs, than to enter into dialogue with it about all these different problems. The Council will clarify these problems in the light of the Gospel and will furnish mankind with the saving resources which the Church has received from its founder under the promptings of the Holy Spirit. It is man himself who must be saved: it is mankind that must be renewed. It is man, therefore, who is the key to this discussion, man considered whole and entire, with body and soul, heart and conscience, mind and will.

II. The people of God believes that it is led by the Spirit of the Lord who fills the whole world. Moved by that faith it tries to discern in the events, the needs, and the longings which it shares with other men of our time, what may be genuine signs of the presence or of the purpose of God. For faith throws a new light on all things and makes known the full ideal which God has set for man, thus guiding the mind towards solutions that are fully human.

In that light the Council intends first of all to assess those values which are most highly prized today and to relate them to their divine source. For such values, in so far as they stem from the natural talents given to man by God, are exceedingly good. Not seldom, however, owing to corruption of the human heart, they are distorted through lack of due order, so that they need to be purified.

Introduction

We have reflected on the Church in prayer *(Sacrosanctum*

54

Concilium), on the Church listening to the Word *(Dei Verbum)* and on the Church as mystery and communion *(Lumen gentium).* We now come to reflect on the image of the Church presented in the dogmatic constitution *Gaudium et spes,* the Church as a sign and an instrument of unity.

The canticle which describes Isaiah's vision will introduce our meditation.

> It shall come to pass in the latter days that the mountain of the house of the Lord shall be raised above the hills; and all the nations shall flow to it, and many peoples shall come, and say: 'Come, let us go up to the mountain of the Lord, to the house of the God of Jacob; that he may teach us his ways and that we may walk in his paths.' For out of Zion shall go forth the law, and the word of the Lord from Jerusalem. He shall judge between the nations, and shall decide for many peoples; and they shall beat their swords into ploughshares, and their spears into pruning hooks; nation shall not lift up sword against nation neither shall they learn war any more. O, house of Jacob, come, let us walk in the light of Lord *(2:2-5).*

It is probable that Isaiah had this vision while watching the people going up to the Temple for the celebration of a Jewish festival. It is helpful to underline some of the images described by the prophet.

The first image is that of *a very high mountain:* on it stands the *temple,* and mountain and temple reach the sky. The second image is of a *stream of people* climbing towards the peak of the mountain. This indicates that the real movement of history is upwards, drawn by the mysterious temple — not a lazy downward descent into the swamps!

Then *sounds* are heard: it is a *psalm of ascent* which the Israelites sang as they went up to the temple. We can think in anticipation of the hymns we shall sing during our forthcoming diocesan pilgrimage to Jerusalem.

In the Canticle we have the image of *the ways of the Lord* which become *the ways of man.* Mankind treads on God's paths.

Finally we have the image of the contrast between the *instruments of peace* and the *instruments of war:* swords/ploughshares, spears/pruning hooks. Situations of conflict are surmounted by peace.

While we slowly pray the prophetic piece, let us ask the Lord to give us the grace of commitment to this appealing vision of the meaning of history.

2. While the theme of our reflection is simple there is some risk of obscuring it with complicated phrases. For this reason perhaps the most convenient way to proceed is to answer the following question: *why does our Holy Father John Paul II undertake such frequent and arduous journeys all over the world?* Because as the head of the Church, he understands himself to be a *sign* and an *instrument* and therefore an advocate of the unity of all peoples amongst themselves. The Pope lives in the ideal of this unity, as we too should do. The Pope's preoccupation of reaching out to all people, all cultures and all races, is the same preoccupation that lies at the heart of the constitution *Gaudium et spes*.

The document was signed on 7 December 1965, the day of the closing of the Council. A great number of themes are dealt with: the dignity of marriage and of the family; culture; economic and social life; peace and war; the political community; the dignity of the human person and of the human community. In the same way, during his many journeys all over the world the Pope speaks of the family, of war and peace, of ecumenism and of dialogue between religions and of unity between peoples.

In all of this what is being underlined is the fact that the Church is a *sign and an instrument of the unity of the human race*.

— In the first place we will endeavour to understand what the *unity* of the human race might mean.
— Then we will ask, how are we to interpret the history of our day-to-day lives so that they may be integrated into that great movement of history leading on to the fullness of unity of the human race.
— Finally we will examine the relationship between this and our task of building up the local Church, in parishes, in parish councils and in the diocese.

The unity of the human race
Gaudium et spes takes its inspiration from the dogmatic constitution *Lumen gentium* and in particular from the following phrase: 'The

56

Church is in Christ as a sacrament (a powerful, sacred and mysterious reality) that is a sign and instrument of our intimate union with God and of the unity of the entire human race' (LG n. 1).

A *sign* means that it signifies: *instrument* means that it effects through the power of God. What does it signify and what does it effect? Man's intimate union with God and the unity of all humanity. This is the reality which we are called on to contemplate.

We can for example contemplate this reality in the image provided in the vision of Isaiah: a great city, a splendid temple on a high mountain and in this temple all men come together to listen to the Word and to observe the law. The ideal is a humanity in which all are called to come together, to feel that they are brothers and sisters, to live in communion.

Look at it in another way. During the previous meetings we spoke about the Church as she is in herself (the Church which prays, which listens and which is mystery totally relative to Jesus). Now, however, we are examining the Church in relation to humanity. Our contention is that *the Church exists so that humanity may be one*. The Church is mystery and communion so that humanity may understand its vocation to unity.

Through this image from Isaiah we can anticipate the end state of history, the goal and the purpose of history: We are all part of this history which is the history of a journey towards unity. Nor are we speaking only of that perfect unity, the Kingdom of God, when Christ will hand over the Kingdom to his father. No, that unity is coming into being here and now because the Church is *already* the sign and the instrument of this unity. The Church is therefore responsible for that unity which is already taking place; equally the Church has to see to it that the entire world becomes one.

A second image that we may find useful is that which is found in the Apocalypse (21:22): A city descends from on high, a city in which there is no longer mourning or weeping or tears because God is with us; God will be with us.

It is this vision of unity that gives meaning and significance to the historical journey of humanity; it is already like a stamp on our daily history, because we have all been called upon to live it.

Yet another image is presented in *Lumen gentium:* Christ raised up from the earth on the cross; he draws all men to himself and through the power of the Holy Spirit forms his body, which is the Church, as a universal sacrament of salvation; Christ works continuously in the world to bring all to the Church and through her to bring them to a close union with himself. The unifying actions of Christ are effected in humanity through the mediation of the Church and of the Spirit.

To summarise these images: the eternal message of the Council is the following: *the unity of all people in Christ according to God's plan.* It is God's wish that all be his children and brothers and sisters to each other by sharing the life and destiny of Jesus. The Church is the community of those who, through God's grace, have understood this, who commit themselves to Jesus and in so doing achieve the fullness of their humanity. They are then the historic sign and the prophetic anticipation, the blessed seed of an entire humanity reunited in Christ in God's time and according to his will and plan.

The Church is therefore sent to proclaim this message to every human being. If we reread *Gaudium et spes* with this central idea in mind we will become more acutely aware of the repeated references to the unity of human society, a unity that is already taking place in the various manifestations of social, political and cultural solidarity which are drawing people ever closer together.

> The accelerated pace of history is such that one can scarcely keep abreast of it. The destiny of the human race is viewed as a complete whole, no longer, as it were, in the particular histories of various peoples: now it merges into a complete whole (*Gaudium et spes* n.5).

This is human history. It is worked out in conflict. We struggle against sin. We struggle against all kinds of obstacles placed in the way by Satan, the enemy of humankind, against death and the inclination towards death, division, confusion and its allies — power, opulence, need for prestige — all hampering our moves towards unity. But these obstacles will not stop our onward journey towards unity because it is already inserted into Christ crucified and risen from the dead and because each one's destiny and the destiny of all humanity are thus marked with this seal.

This single vision of history is confirmed many times by our renewed efforts — though they falter and fail from time to time — to know and understand each other, to find common ground and to work together. It is a foretaste of that intimate union to which God, in Christ, calls the entire human race:

> ...the body of a new human family grows, foreshadowing in some way the age which is to come. That is why, although we must be careful to distinguish earthly progress clearly from the increase of the kingdom of Christ, such progress is of vital concern to the kingdom of God (*Gaudium et spes* n.39).

The triple groaning *(Romans 8:18-27)*

What then might help us to see in our own little daily history, that larger movement that is guiding all history and humanity towards Christ, Lord and Judge? The answer is to be found in Paul's letter to the Romans (8:18-27) where he speaks of a triple groaning.

— the groaning of creation: 'we know that the whole of creation has been groaning in travail together until now...'

— our groaning: 'but we ourselves who have the first fruits of the Spirit groan inwardly as we wait for adoption as sons ...'

— the groaning of the Spirit: 'The Spirit himself intercedes for us with sighs too deep for words ...'

What lies behind this image of groaning or sighing? Groaning or sighing is the expression of a deeply felt but partially repressed desire, that nevertheless cannot be held back; it springs from within us, and represents something very deep indeed.

In the passage the groan represents the desire for the revelation of the fullness of unity, the end state of history.

1. In the first instance the Apostle sees physical creation as groaning: but it is in culture, in society, in peoples and their development, in the history of nations and in wars. An attentive reading of history will yield up this understanding.

2. Then St Paul considers our groaning. We are believers in Jesus Christ, we contemplate him in his Gospel, we are led by the Spirit in prayer and thus are enabled to voice the need for unity amongst people. In this our model is John Paul II who is the voice proclaiming, crying out humanity's need for unity;

he says clearly that if we do not achieve this unity the year 2000 will bring calamity! If you cannot come to some understanding among yourselves there will be no survival! This is the sigh of a believer, of one who feels the power of the Gospel and the force for unity exerted by the resurrection of Jesus, and who then proclaims this awareness to those around.

3. This sigh is sustained by the sigh of the Spirit, who, penetrating the universe and the hearts of Christians, inspires them with a yearning for the Kingdom and a foretaste of the fullness of God's reign, and leads them on their journey with that certitude. This is how the Spirit of God helps us to discern the ways of God and the historic journey of humanity towards the unity of the Kingdom. As Church we are then to be at the disposal of that unity, its sign, its sacrament and its instrument.

Our responsibilities

What practical conclusions should be drawn from this? We are certainly not called to travel the world to preach the unity of all humanity, to make people understand that all things are embraced by the mystery of the cross and the resurrection of Christ. It appears to me that we have four responsibilities. I will explain them so that everyone can then see how they apply personally.

Firstly, we must move out from restricted visions of reality. A Christian is not really a Christian if he does not open his heart to the groaning of all creation and to the sighs of the Holy Spirit.

Too often our communities are inward looking, navel gazing, bent on petty thoughts about trivia, without broadening their vision to encompass the immensity of what we are and our responsibility, both part of the unity of the human race.

Secondly, do we have a deep desire for this unity? Do we, even from time to time, reflect on the mystery of unity? For example, during adoration of the Blessed Sacrament do I endeavour to see the Sacred Host as the centre of the world? Do I endeavour to see around the Host all humanity, those whom I know or do not know? Do I live feel, live and reflect on this unity?

Thirdly, where and how do we promote unity? The answer is very simple. We promote it every time we create an opportunity, however small, of bringing about unity, gestures and actions that accomplish unity. Equally we destroy unity every time, no matter in how small a way, we bring about divisions, lack of respect for others, defeatism, scepticism towards our environment or the Church, negative and unfounded judgements of others. Positive judgements promote unity as does encouragement, invitations to do things and praise for what others achieve. The cultivation of unity means carrying out small acts of unity and avoiding what destroys it.

Fourthly, does our pastoral council promote unity? Is it merely a decision-making forum or does it also afford us an opportunity for reflecting on the totality of the wider plan of salvation? Arising from this reflection are we led to reflect on the unity of the parish community which we are called on to build?

I would like to add a further very brief reflection, bearing also in mind the goal which the Holy Father has for his journeys: the unity of the human race increases in proportion to the growth in ecumenism.

'We are also mindful that the unity of Christians is today awaited and longed for by many non-believers. For the more this unity is realised in truth and charity under the powerful impulse of the Holy Spirit, the more it will be the harbinger of unity and peace throughout the whole world' (*Gaudium et spes,* n.92).

Ecumenical action is therefore an occasion of unity for the entire universe.
'O Lord enlighten us during our Eucharistic adoration; make us instruments and servants of that unity of the human race which is the unity of humanity with God, and the fullness of the revelation of your divine glory'.

5

THE MISSIONARY CHURCH

From Revelation *(4:11; 5:9.10.12.13)*
Worthy art thou, O Lord and God
*   to receive glory and honour and power,*
For thou didst create all things,
and by thy will they existed and were created.

Worthy art thou to take the scroll
*   and to open its seals,*
for thou wast slain and by thy blood
*   didst ransom men for God*
from every tribe and tongue and people and nation
*   and hast made them*
a kingdom and priests to our God
*   and they shall reign on earth.*

Worthy is the lamb who was slain, to receive power and wealth
*   and wisdom*
and might and honour and glory and blessing!

To him who sits upon the throne and to the Lamb be blessing
*   and honour*
and glory and might for ever and ever!

From the Letter to the Philippians *(1:3-6)*
I thank my God in all my remembrance of you, always in every prayer
of mine for you all making my prayer with joy, thankful for your partnership
in the Gospel from the first day until now. And I am sure that he who
began a good work in you will bring it to completion at the day of Jesus
Christ.

From Matthew's Gospel *(28:16-20)*
*Now the eleven disciples went to Galilee, to the mountain to which Jesus
had directed them. And when they saw him they worshipped him; but
some doubted. And Jesus came and said to them, 'All authority in heaven
and on earth has been given to me. Go therefore and make disciples of
all nations, baptising them in the name of the Father and of the Son and
of the Holy Spirit, teaching them to observe all that I have commanded
you; and lo, I am with you always, to the close of the age'.*

From the Decree on the Missionary Activity of the Church, *Ad gentes* (nn. 1 and 2)

*1.   In the present state of things which gives rise to a new situation for
mankind, the Church, the salt of the earth and the light of the world (cf.
Mt 5:13-14), is even more urgently called upon to save and renew every
creature, so that all things might be restored in Christ, and so that in him
men might form one family and one people of God.*

*2.   The Church on earth is by its very nature missionary since, according
to the plan of the Father, it has its origin in the mission of the Son and
the Holy Spirit.*

From the Decree on the Apostolate of the Laity, *Apostolicam actuositatem,* (n.9)

*9.   The lay apostolate, in all its many aspects, is exercised both in the
Church and in the world. In either case different fields of apostolic action
are open to the laity. We propose to mention here the chief among them:
Church communities, the family, the young, the social environment, national
and international spheres. Since in our days women are taking an
increasingly active share in the whole life of society, it is very important
that their participation in the various sectors of the Church's apostolate
should likewise develop.*

We chose the canticle from the Apocalypse because of its
description of the universality of salvation: 'Men from every
tribe, tongue, people and nation'. The first two verses are a hymn
of praise to God who is seated on his throne and who has created
all things:

'Worthy art thou, Our Lord and God, to receive glory and
honour and power, for thou didst create all things and by thy
will they existed and were created'.

64

In the subsequent verses we find a canticle to Jesus, cornerstone and Lord of history who ransomed all people, making them into a universal kingdom; for this he is praised by hosts of angels and by all living creatures:

'worthy art thou to take the scroll and to open its seals. For thou wast slain and by thy blood didst ransom men for God.

From every tribe and tongue and people and nation'.

Let us then bring ourselves to the contemplation of the Church's universal mission: 'Grant us Lord to sing your praise with a heart that is catholic and universal; grant that, in true missionary spirit, we may enter into God's plan which embraces all times and all places. From this cathedral we reach out to the entire universe which you have redeemed, and which you call to yourself through the work of your Church'.

Background to our meditation: the missionary nature of the Church

The background of our meditation this evening is clearly expressed in the beginning of the Conciliar Decree on the Church's Missionary Activity, *Ad gentes*:

In the present state of things which gives rise to a new situation for mankind the Church, the salt of the earth and the light of the world (cf. Mt 5:13-14), is even more urgently called upon to save and renew every creature, so that all things might be restored in Christ, and so that in him men might form one family and one people of God ... The Church on earth is by its very nature missionary since, according to the plan of the Father, it has its origin in the mission of the Son and Holy Spirit.

Christ wishes to recapitulate all things in himself; men and women ought to constitute one family, one people in God. This is the universal mission of Jesus. We spoke of this at some length when we commented on *Gaudium et spes:* the unity of the human race is the goal of God's plan.

What then is the role of the Church, salt of the earth and light of the world? Its mission, in relation to the unity of humanity in Christ, is instrumental and subordinate. The Church is called on to fulfil its mission by saving and renewing every creature.

Ad gentes declares that this mission is now more urgent than ever because of the present state of society. To understand this last, we can refer again to the words of John Paul II, in speaking frequently about the approach of the year 2000; it is an extraordinary phase in human history when, unlike ever before, there is enormous scope for the unity of humanity through means of communication, knowledge, exchange and interdependence; at the same time, again as never before, humanity runs the risk of self-destruction.

We now stand at a critical turning point in the history of humanity. The Church must therefore examine its missionary calling with renewed urgency so that all things may be recapitulated in Christ. Here we have the background to all our actions and to all our decisions: we are part of a great historic moment in the action of Christ, of him who holds the book of history in his hands and who draws to himself the entirety of universal history.

The context of our meditation: collaboration of the laity
We find the immediate context for our meditation in an extract from the Conciliar Decree on the Apostolate of the Laity.

> The lay apostolate, in all its many aspects, is exercised both in the Church and in the world. In either case different fields of apostolic action are open to the laity. We propose to mention here the chief among them: Church communities, the family, the young, the social environment, national and international spheres. Since in our days women are taking an increasingly active share in the whole life of society, it is very important that their participation in the various sectors of the Church's apostolate should likewise develop' (*Apostolicam Actuositatem,* n.9).

The immediate context is the collaboration of the laity in this universal mission. Lay people are a vital part of the missionary movement of the Church and the Council also rightly underlines the importance of the participation of women in this apostolate.

We might then ask ourselves: against the background of the universal mission of Christ and of the Church, and taking into account the immediate context of the role of the laity, what is the function of the pastoral council? Our pastoral councils are an active instrument; they are a means in giving expression to the missionary role of the Church here and now. They are not an adjunct, a secondary stratum, but are rather an intimate part of God's plan. For this reason, during the course of our reflections this year, I have underlined the importance of preparing lay people for membership of the pastoral councils. In this I am convinced that we have the key to a new phase in the missionary path of the Church and of the diocese.

Prayer of the bishop

I would now like to read, indeed with a certain amount of emotion, that wonderful prayer which we find at the beginning of Paul's letter to the Philippians. I like to call it 'the bishop's prayer for his lay people'. So that you may share my feeling for this piece of writing I have scanned the verses into the eight component parts that go to make up the theme.

> I thank my God
> in all my remembrances of you
> always in every prayer of mine for you all
> making my prayer with joy,
> Thankful for your partnership in the Gospel,
> from the first day until now,
> And I am sure
> that he who began a good work in you
> will bring it to completion at the day of
> Jesus Christ.

Bearing in mind then the scansion of this outburst of prayer and of testimony by Paul, we note that the central verse is *'thankful for your partnership in the Gospel';* thus the centre of the bishop's prayer is thankfulness for your cooperation in spreading the Gospel, for the cooperation of lay men and women. The Greek text has, in effect, a shorter and more meaningful expression — 'your communion, your *"koinonia"* in the Gospel.'

What is the meaning of this phrase, 'your communion in the Gospel', which was the reason for the great prayer and joy of the Apostle? In the first instance it is the ready *welcome* of the Gospel by the citizens of Philippi. It was the first of the Greek cities to be evangelised by Paul. But as well as acceptance there is also the active participation of these recently converted laity in the spreading of the Gospel. Because of lack of historical detail we do not know exactly what they did, but we do know, from the Acts, some of the moving incidents that took place and, especially, the origin of this evangelisation.

Paul began his preaching in the synagogue at Philippi where he was unknown to all. No doubt he spoke with a certain amount of fear and trepidation. The account in the Acts tells us that one of those who heard the preaching was a women called Lydia (see *Acts 16:14*). She was from Asia Minor and traded in purple goods. The business was profitable and enabled her to live at a reasonably high standard. The Acts goes on to describe how the Lord opened her heart so that she and her household were baptised.

Right from the first day she began to take care of the missionaries: 'If you have judged me to be faithful to the Lord, come to my house and stay' *(Acts 16:15)*. The words indicate great humility and decisiveness. In fact the text goes on to say that 'she prevailed upon us' — indicating Lydia's energetic approach. She had believed with all her heart and now she was determined that she would take care of the mission and that her home should become its centre.

The first to be evangelised and the first evangeliser of Philippi was therefore a woman. We know that Paul had to leave the city quite soon afterwards — it was perhaps a question of a few weeks later — but the fledgling community already had lay members who promoted the service of the Gospel.

In the final chapter of the letter to the Philippians, Paul mentions two other helpers, again both women. 'I entreat you Euodia and I entreat Syntyche ... who have laboured side by side with me in the Gospel ...' *(Phil 4:2-3)*. For the sake of honesty we should mention that what Paul entreats them to do is 'to agree in the Lord'. He suggests that even in the early Christian community harmony between collaborators was not always easy to achieve. Paul mentions by name these persons who were close to him and touches lightly on their disagreement. He continues with the names of his other helpers 'whose names are in the book of life'.

The Christian community at Philippi began about the year 50-51. Writing to them some years later, Paul still remembers with emotion the enthusiasm and courage of that simple people:

You have cooperated with me from the first day, and you have never tired. In the same letter *(4:18)* he speaks of the gifts sent to him in prison in Rome. The community at Philippi were anxious to ease Paul's lot while in prison. This act of love and affection was an enormous source of joy for Paul. After all, in a period of difficult communications these gifts came to him from the other side of the Mediterranean.

There is a wealth of emotion in the phrase *'I thank my God'*. It almost seems affected, as if the Lord were his alone. Perhaps the emotional intensity is that of the pastor who feels that he is understood by his people, by the lay helpers who have cooperated with him for the sake of the Gospel.

In the other Pauline writings there are a number of acts of thankgiving for lay people and for the response of the community. There is a touching passage from the second letter to the Corinthians, in which Paul speaks of the suffering he had from them, his fears and anxieties for them and adds:

'But God who comforts the downcast, comforted us by the coming of Titus, and not only by his coming but also by the comfort with which he was comforted in you, as he told us of your longing, your mourning, your zeal for me, so that I rejoiced still more' *(2 Cor 7:6-7)*.

The sufferings and joys of his helpers were Paul's own sufferings and joys. This helps us to understand the opening verses of the letter to the Philippians 'I thank my God *in all my remembrance of you'*. I never think of you except with a sense of gratitude, never with regret or bitterness or ill-feeling.

'Always in every prayer of mine for you all, making my prayer with joy', for the cooperation of the laity in the spreading of the Gospel is the very flowering of the Church, the joy of the bishop, a gift from heaven and the very fullness of the Christian life.

Paul is heartened by the strength he derives from this cooperation; it is his interior sustenance and the fact that his people stood by him during his apostolic labours is a guarantee of their future cooperation *'I am sure* (I feel in my heart, because I know you, I love you, and I know God loves you) *that he who began a good work in you will bring it to completion in the day of Jesus Christ.'* His hope is that cooperation by lay people, not only those who were known to him but throughout the entire Church, would grow 'until the day of Jesus Christ'. This is Paul's prayer; it is the bishop's prayer and, if you like, a witness of my prayer for you. I feel that I share the day, thanksgiving, trust and certainty which Paul cherished for his collaborators. These are my feelings towards all the priests of the diocese and with them towards all our lay helpers.

This is the only way in which the Church can become missionary and broaden its sphere of influence in the present day. It is the only way for the Church to overcome the commonplace, the routine and the adherence to the status quo so that she may shine forth according to Christ's grand plan for unity which he handed down to each of us from the cross. Each one of us, here and now in this year (1986) has a responsibility towards past generations as well as a responsibility for future generations.

Concluding questions

By way of conclusion let me raise some questions both for you and for your communities: for pastoral council members, for helpers, for educators, for catechists, those who are closely involved in Church action.

1. How do I live out in my daily life that broad vision that envisages the goal of the pilgrim Church? How do I live out tht background, which is the unity of the entire human race in Christ. Can my community see beyond the immediate, is its vision broad enough to encompass the whole world? Are these broader perspectives present in our daily discussions, in facing up to problems, in the reflections that take place in my group or in my pastoral council? If we still fall short of this ideal, how much more do we need to turn to prayer?

2. Do I feel the joy of cooperation in spreading the Gospel, the joy Paul spoke about? Is this joy felt in my group, by the helpers whom I know? Do we work joyfully or simply do things because they have to be done?

3. Do I share Paul's conviction that he who began the good work in us will bring it to a conclusion? Do I place trust in the Lord who works in us? Do I feel that it is God who guides us and, as a result, do we trust in him as a group, a parish, a pastoral council?

4. Finally, the most imporant question: What is Jesus asking me to do in relation to these realities? What can I do in my own

environment to promote an awareness of the background of universality, to make present the joy of cooperation in the Gospel, and to instil confidence in God who in these difficult times continues to guide us? In asking what Jesus wants you to do you might review the six areas of apostolic activity which we have mentioned: the community of the Church, the family, youth, the social environment and national and international policy.

Let us think in particular of young people, of school and of the teaching of religion. What is Jesus asking me to do in the coming months so that horizons may be broadened within the group, within the pastoral council, in my group and in my own environment, so that people may strive joyfully and confidently to have a proper understanding of their obligations, of their commitments and of God's call.

Let us kneel before the crucifix: 'Lord you who have done so much for me, what are you asking me to do for you?'

6

THE HOLINESS OF THE CHURCH

From the Acts of the Apostles *(9:31)*
So the Church throughout all Judaea and Galilee and Samaria had peace and was built up; and walking in the fear of the Lord and in the comfort of the Holy Spirit it was multiplied.

From the dogmatic constitution on the Church, *Lumen gentium* (nn. 38 and 40)
38. Each individual layman must be a witness before the world to the resurrection and life of the Lord Jesus, and a sign of the living God. All together, and each one to the best of his ability, must nourish the world with spiritual fruits (cf. Gal. 5:22). They must diffuse in the world the spirit which animates those poor, meek and peace-makers whom the Lord in the Gospel proclaimed blessed (cf. Mt 5:3-9). In a word: what the soul is in the body, let Christians be in the world!

40. The Lord Jesus, divine teacher and model of all perfection, preached holiness of life (of which he is the author and maker) to each and every one of his disciples without distinction: 'you, therefore, must be perfect, as your heavenly Father is perfect' (Mt 5:48). For he sent the Holy Spirit to all to move them interiorly to love God with their whole heart, with their whole soul, with their whole understanding and with their whole strength (cf. Mk 12:30) and to love one another as Christ loved them (cf. Jn 13:34; 15:12) ...
It is therefore quite clear to everybody that all Christians in whatever state or walk of life are called to the fullness of Christian life and to the perfection of love, and by this holiness a more human manner of life is

fostered also in earthly society. In order to reach this perfection the faithful should use the strength dealt out to them by Christ's gift so that, following in his footsteps and conformed to his image, doing the will of God in everything, they may wholeheartedly devote themselves to the glory of God and to the service of their neighbour. Thus the holiness of the People of God will grow in fruitful abundance, as is clearly shown in the history of the Church through the life of so many saints.

Those moments of silence which are the high point of all our meetings – for it is then that the Lord speaks to us and invites us to undertake something for him — those moments are of particular importance this evening. We are about to reflect on the *holiness of the Church*, desiring to understand the image of Church that the Lord is calling on us to construct.

The Church is holy not only because of its many saints. The dogmatic constitution *Lumen gentium* draws attention to the fact that the holiness of the Church is a challenge for each and every individual, and challenges us as members of pastoral councils.

I will reread these texts aloud to show how in all their simplicity and richness they provide us with the basic elements of sanctity: its *diffusion,* its *norm* and *rule,* its *root,* then its *fruits,* its *exercise* and, lastly, its *final goal.*

Fundamental elements of ecclesial holiness

In the first place the *diffusion* of holiness: '*Each* individual layperson must be a witness before the world to the resurrection and life of the Lord Jesus, and a sign of the living God. *All* together and each one to the best of his ability must nourish the world with spiritual fruits (cf. *Gal. 5:22*). They must diffuse in the world the spirit which animates those poor, meek and peacemakers whom the Lord in the Gospel proclaimed blessed *(cf. Mt 5:3-9)* — LG 38.

Or again: 'the Lord Jesus, divine teacher and model of all perfection, preached holiness of life (of which he is the author and maker) to each and everyone of his disciples without distinction … he sent the Holy Spirit to *all* …'

It is therefore quite clear to everybody that *all* Christians, in whatever state or walk of life, are called to the fullness of Christian life and to the perfection of love …' — LG 40.

Nobody is excluded from the call to the perfection of charity,

74

to the fullness of the Christian life and nobody is excused for reasons of age — I'm too young!, I'm too old! — or for reasons of inability to follow the way of the Spirit. *Each and every one* of us can be saints.

The rule of sanctity is also expressed in LG 40: 'You therefore must be *perfect* as your heavenly Father is perfect'. This is a synthesis of Christian morality: to be holy, to be perfect means to be *like* God, to imitate God. The *'being like God'* is explained in the text 'following in Christ's footsteps and conformed to his image'. If we follow the example of Jesus we will achieve sanctity. The Christian vocation consists in following the example of Jesus Son of God in a concrete fashion and in living as he lived. Every Christian has the grace and the strength to do this.

The question naturally arises: is this really possible? Will we really succeed in doing what is asked of us? The dogmatic constitution affirms that the *root* and the *origin* of holiness is not within ourselves because we cannot achieve it of ourselves. 'For he sent *the Holy Spirit to all to move them* interiorly to love God with their whole heart ... and to love one another as Christ loved them.' Our good will, our courage, the good education we have received or, indeed, a moment of conversion do not of themselves constitute holiness. It is the Holy Spirit from within our hearts that allows us to love God with our whole mind and our neighbour with all our strength. It is the Holy Spirit that makes each one of us into a saint: each one of us is, therefore, holy because in each one of us the Spirit of the Lord dwells, or could dwell, or wishes to dwell.

It seems most opportune that we should be reflecting on this theme on the feast of the Ascension. Forty days have passed since Easter and we are now preparing for Pentecost which will celebrate the outpouring of the Spirit on the early Church and one each of the disciples. The root of holiness is not to be found in our good intentions, in our attentive readings nor in our meditations, pious devotions or sacrifices. All these things are, however, useful and are from the Holy Spirit who is within us and brings about Christian holiness in us.

The human and historical *fruits* are clearly described: 'and by this holiness a more human manner of life is fostered also in earthly society' (LG 40). Saints irradiate a more human standard of life on this earth and, thanks to them, humanity becomes more human. Another fruit is mentioned where it is said that every Christian 'must nourish the world with spiritual fruits and diffuse in it the spirit of the gospel (LG 38).' Holiness is the world's nourishment and without it the world would die of hunger, hunger for meaning. Without holiness the world would no longer know the reason for its existence, it would no longer know what it is about. Holiness strengthens and nourishes the world, spreading in it the spirit of the beatitudes, the spirit of meekness, of poverty and of peace. 'In a word what the soul is in the body let Christians be in the world' (LG 38) in order to give the world life, strength and hope.

All believers, to the extent to which they allow the Holy Spirit to work in them, become the soul of their environment, of the reality that surrounds them, of their group, because the Holy Spirit diffuses holiness everywhere.

In practical terms what does the saintly Christian do? The *exercise* of holiness is described in these terms: 'each individual layman must be a witness before the world to the resurrection and life of the Lord Jesus' (LG 38). By bearing witness to the presence 'of the living God' (LG 38), by bearing witness to the resurrection and life of the Lord Jesus through the newness of their own lives, Christians nourish the hope and love of the world.

Finally, the *ultimate goal* of holiness is to construct a people of saints who will sing of the glory of God to the world: 'the holiness of the people of God will grow in fruitful abundance ...'. All 'will wholeheartedly devote themselves to the glory of God and to the service of their neighbour' (LG 40).

A holy Church

The marvellous statements of the Council are one thing. A degree of scepticism remains and the question arises: will this actually happen historically in the Church?

The answer is to be found in the very short passage of Acts: 'So the Church, throughout all Judaea and Galilee and Samaria had peace and was built up; and walking in the fear of the Lord and in the comfort of the Holy Spirit it was multiplied' *(9:31)*.

This is a description of a holy Church. At that period the early Church lived out its joy, its fullness and its holiness. Let us try further to understand this text, beginning with its conclusion: '...*in the comfort of the Holy Spirit*'. It was a Church that experienced the fullness of the Holy Spirit who, as we have said, gave rise to her holiness. The Spirit comforted her, consoled her and encouraged her rather as Jesus did for the disciples at Emmaus.

The Church was *filled totally* with this comfort; it experienced the fullness of the Spirit. Some of the typical sayings of St Paul come to mind: 'I am filled with comfort. With all our affliction, I am overjoyed' *(2 Cor 7:4)*. Though suffering greatly the Apostle was filled to overflowing with consolation; this is characteristic of the holiness of the Church. Or again we remember Paul in the depths of a prison; wounded, lacerated and in chains: 'about midnight Paul and Silas were praying and singing hymns to God' *(Acts 16:25)*.

This same consolation in the midst of suffering is today being experienced in ways that at times seem miraculous and that continue to reveal the presence of the Spirit ready to comfort and sanctify his Church. I could cite a number of examples from among those whom I knew in a real prison, but I would prefer to give an example of someone imprisoned by illness. Allow me to read from a letter written by Benedetta Bianchi Porro who died at the age of twenty-seven. This year (1986) is in fact the fiftieth anniversary of her birth. From her adolesence onwards Benedetta's life was one of continuous suffering to the point of blindness, deafness and loss of feeling in her limbs. She became virtually unable to communicate. She was really imprisoned. In the final stages of her illness she wrote to a friend: 'My dear friend, sometimes I find myself in his presence empty-handed without having even crumbs. At times I suffer intolerably. I wish that it were all over; at times I ask that I may suffer even more. There are times when I am unhinged, on a shaky ladder with nothing to hold on to, wandering and unable to get up … I prayed, I spoke to God; I laid bare my fears to him and once again I heard the voice of the Father. Thirsting I ran to be comforted; it was he; I was hearing him again, I had found him again. What relief! With him I feel I can go far, to the end of the earth if it be his wish. I do not need to stop, nor do I need to rest. I have found the Lord again, I have reheard his voice and our conversation was sweet and gentle.'

Benedetta was no doubt filled with the consolation of the Holy Spirit.

77

'The Church, walking in the fear of the Lord ... was multiplied' *(Acts 9:31)*.

The early Church grew numerically — we are told of the newly baptised members — and she also grew in maturity and in faith. She travelled the roads of the world geographically and she walked in holiness because the sense of fullness had expanded her heart.

'The Church had *peace*'. Peace is a characteristic of holiness. It is worth noting that the text adds 'throughout all Judaea and Galilee and Samaria'. These are the three regions covered by Jesus in his journeys and the Church, for she is now Jesus, retreads that same ground and in the peace and joy of the Spirit travels the roads of the entire world.

Concluding questions

As we continue to meditate personally on the texts of *Lumen gentium* and *Acts*, it would be useful to ask ourselves four questions:

1. Do I, even sometimes, feel the *consolation of the Holy Spirit?* As a community — the parish, the religious community, our group — do we feel this fullness of consolation? Or, is it the case that we more often feel a dearth, the anxiety of one who has nothing in hand, a sense of frustration?

Why do we have so much moaning in our communities? Are we convinced that the norm of communion and the normal situation for a Christian community ought to be the fullness of the consolation of the Holy Spirit?

'Jesus, why do we not experience the fullness of the comfort of the Spirit, why are we so closed in on ourselves in sadness and anxiety?'

Or again, 'We thank you, Jesus, for those moments when we experience the fullness of the comfort, and of the consolation of the Holy Spirit'.

2. *Are we growing* in Christian maturity? Is it my experience that the Lord is causing me to grow in faith, in love, in patience and humility? Is our community growing in number, in gifts, and in the range of services it provides? If we are not growing this means that rather than being a Church on the march, we are static, halted in a lay-by.

'Lord grant that we may experience what you want us to do in order to move ahead and to grow'.

3. Do I experience *peace* in spite of the conflicts that surround me? As a community do we experience peace in spite of problems, different viewpoints, fears for the future, many anxieties about the Church and society and so many problems that distress us?

Jesus says 'I give you peace, not as the world gives peace'. This peace is not absence of conflict or of preoccupations. It is rather our participation in the suffering of the world, our sharing in its fears of wars and disasters and of everything that threatens humanity. It is, however, peace in our hearts. One of the characteristics of the Church is that she always maintains the peace of Jesus, even in times of persecution, squalls and tempests. Are we really a Church of peace?

4. The Acts speak of the Church which was in *Judaea, Samaria* and *Galilee*. How do we live the reality of the local Church — the Church in Italy, the Church in Lombardy, the Church of Milan? What is our contribution to the holiness of this Church and what do we do to bring about an increase in her holiness?

'Holy men and women have always been the source and origin of renewal in the most difficult periods of the Church's history. Today, more than ever, we need saints and we should not cease to implore God to raise them up' (*Final Report* of Synod II part 2, A, 4).

May Saints Ambrose and Victor and Charles, and all the holy bishops of Milan intercede for us. May holy religious men and women, the saints who were called to live out the family vocation and all the holy people we have known — may these intercede for us. Above all we rely on the intercession of the Virgin Mary.

'Lord God, Our Father, who revealed yourself to us in Jesus Christ your son, pour out upon us abundantly your Spirit of holiness. We praise you and give you thanks: among all your gifts one alone, the Spirit, is central; among the various ways of serving you, one alone is the Lord; among all our actions you alone, O God, do all things and operate in all things. Grant that our communities may grow and walk in fear of you, Father of life and love. Grant that our communities may experience the fullness of consolation even in the midst of inevitable sufferings. Give us your Spirit of peace and joy, so that on the highways of the world we may spread the spirit of the Gospel and all people may come to recognise you as the one true God and him whom you have sent, Jesus Christ'.

7

THE CHURCH OF CHARITY FOR THE
LIFE OF THE WORLD

(Psalm 127)
Unless the Lord builds the house,
those who build it labour in vain.
Unless the Lord watches over the city,
the watchman stays awake in vain.
It is in vain that you rise up early
and go late to rest,
eating the bread of anxious toil;
for he gives to his beloved sleep.

Lo, sons are a heritage from the Lord,
the fruit of the womb a reward.
Like arrows in the hand of a warrior
are the sons of one's youth.
Happy is the man who has
his quiver full of them!
He shall not be put to shame
when he speaks with his enemies in the gate.

From Luke's Gospel *(19:29-44)*
When he drew near to Bethphage and Bethany, at the mount that is called
Olivet, he sent two of the disciples, saying, 'Go into the village opposite
where on entering you will find a colt tied, on which no one has ever yet
sat; untie it and bring it here. If any one asks you "Why you untying
it?" you shall say this, "The Lord has need of it".' So those who were
sent away and found it as he had told them. And as they were untying

81

the colt, its owners said to them 'Why are you untying the colt?' And they said 'The Lord has need of it'. And they brought it to Jesus, and throwing their garments on the colt they set Jesus upon it. And as he rode along, they spread their garments on the road. And as he was now drawing near, at the descent of the Mount of Olives, the whole multitude of the disciples began to rejoice and praise God with a loud voice for all the mighty works that they had seen, saying, 'Blessed is the King who comes in the name of the Lord! Peace in heaven and glory in the highest!' And some of the Pharisees in the multitude said to him, 'Teacher rebuke your disciples'. He answered, 'I tell you, if these were silent, the very stones would cry out.'

And when he drew near and saw the city he wept over it, saying, 'Would that even today you knew the things that make for peace! But now they are hid from your eyes. For the days shall come upon you, when your enemies will cast up a bank about you and surround you, and hem you in on every side, and dash you to the ground, you and your children within you, and they will not leave one stone upon another in you; because you did not know the time of your visitation.'

From the Dogmatic Constitution on the Church, *Lumen gentium* (n.9)

That messianic people has as its head Christ, 'who was delivered up for our sins and rose again for our justification' (Rom 4:25), and now, having acquired the name which is above all names, reigns gloriously in heaven. The state of this people is that of the dignity and freedom of the sons of God, in whose hearts the Holy Spirit dwells as in a temple. Its law is the new commandment to love as Christ loved us (cf. Jn 13:34). Its destiny is the kingdom of God which has been begun by God himself on earth and which must be further extended until it is brought to perfection by him at the end of time when Christ our life (cf. Col 3:4) will appear and 'creation itself also will be delivered from its slavery to corruption into the freedom of the glory of the sons of God' (Rom. 8:21). Hence that messianic people, although it does not actually include all men, and at times may appear as a small flock, is however, a most sure seed of unity, hope and salvation for the whole human race. Established by Christ as a communion of life, love and truth, it is taken up by him also as the instrument for the salvation of all; as the light of the world and the salt of the earth (cf. Mt 5:13-16) it is sent forth into the whole world.

As Israel, according to the flesh which wandered in the desert already called the Church of God (2 Esd 13:1; cf. Num 20:4 Deut 23:1 ff), so too, the new Israel, which advances in this present era in search of a future and permanent city (cf. Heb. 13:14), is called the Church of Christ (cf. Mt 16:18). It is Christ indeed who has purchased it with his own blood (cf. Acts 20:28); he has filled it with his Spirit; he has provided means adapted to its visible and social union. All those, who in faith look towards Jesus, the author of salvation and the principle of unity and peace, God has gathered together and established as the Church, that it may be for each and everyone the visible sacrament of this saving unity. Destined to extend to all regions of the earth, it enters into human history though it transcends at once all times and all racial boundaries. Advancing through trials and tribulations, the Church is strengthened by God's grace, promised to her by the Lord so that she may not waver from perfect fidelity but remain the worthy bride of the Lord, ceaselessly renewing herself through the action of the Holy Spirit, until, through the cross, she may attain to that light which knows no setting.

Introduction

This is an important contemplative time for the Church. It is the vigil of the feast of the Sacred Heart — a night of vigil in union with the Heart of Jesus.

It is also the last of our first Thursday of the month meetings. Two different streams of activity come together — one, our meetings here in the cathedral which have been essentially for members of the pastoral councils, and the other is represented by the various initiatives on behalf of the youth of the diocese which have been taking place in various parts of the diocese. The very confluence of these two streams is not without turbulence and though there are moments of meditative cohesion, it is not easy to unify them.

I believe however that the sentiments of thanksgiving as expressed in Psalm 127 can unify both streams:

'O Lord we thank you for the wonders we have witnessed during this year and for the gifts you have showered on us during our monthly meetings.

We praise you and give you thanks for the graces bestowed on our youth who in their thousands have been meeting in the various churches of the diocese. We thank you for having built the house and we have not worked or watched in vain.

You have given us the bread of your Word during these meditations: we are your children, fruit of your womb. Grant that we may comprehend the mystery of your Church and your people'.

Two themes emerge. One is a study of the image of the Church portrayed in Vatican II, and we will contemplate her as the people of God. The other is the Church of charity. Our youth have reflected on the 'pathways' of charity and the pathway we will follow this evening is charity in politics. Our readings from *Lumen gentium* and from the Gospel of Luke correspond, in a certain way, to our chosen themes.

One reading develops the theme of the people of God, while in the Gospel we find Jesus confronting his city, i.e. political reality. Let us try to read the two passages gather their values.

Reading of *Lumen gentium*, (n.9): The people of God
Our text from *Lumen gentium* is found in the second chapter of the Constitution:

1. It represents the Council's major step forward in Ecclesiology, i.e. our understanding of the Church. Various images of the Church are put forward in chapter 1 which deals with the mystery of the Church: the Church as flock, the field of God, God's building, the heavenly Jerusalem, our mother, spouse of the Lamb, mystical Body.

The unifying theme in the second chapter is the Church as the people of God. The subsequent chapters deal with specific aspects, such as the hierarchy, the laity and religious, in order to draw our attention to various ways of considering unity and the communion of believers within the Church and, in particular, to underline the participation of the laity in the full pilgrimage of the people of God.

The second chapter, from which we have read two very basic passages which are among the most marvellous pages of Vatican II, is of fundamental importance. We find a description of the messianic people and its head; our condition, the laws which bind us, our aim, our mission and our final goal are all described.

This is a very dense and rich piece of writing. It speaks about what we are — Pope, priests, bishops, religious, laity, children, old people, families — we are this reality; all are equal here; all share in the same dignity, liberty, charity and mission.

This extract should be read with wonder, avoiding any restricted reading. If we give it a reductionist, or restricted reading (with one eye only) we will see the people of God merely in the historic evolution, in its temporal manifestation, that is earth-bound and time-bound in history. We must, as the text itself invites us, broaden our horizons: the people of God has as its head Christ, who is reigning gloriously in heaven.

The people of God is not however limited to us here and now. It is that immense throng who look to Christ as their head. It thus includes Mary, the apostles, the saints and the whole Church of all times.

The synod warns against the danger of substituting one unilateral view of the Church (a purely hierarchical structure) with another, equally unilateral definition (a purely sociological vision). Jesus is always present in the Church, and lives in it as the Risen One. The pilgrim Church on earth is already a messianic people and anticipates within herself the new creation.

We must have this vision if we are to understand the people of God: it is the people of God here and now on the way, on a journey, but at the same time we are part of the heavenly Church. Thus the heavenly Church is descending from above, becoming part of history and giving life to history.

Cardinal Henri de Lubac has the following comment on our extract from *Lumen gentium:* 'The people of God, guided from generation to generation towards the heavenly Jerusalem is already mystically one with Christ; it is a grand collective march towards unity'. Called together by the first preaching of the Gospel, the people of God draws the human race to itself and sets out towards the final unity of humanity in Christ, the consummation of the universe in God; all this is now taking place in us.

The Fathers of the Church often referred to this reality; for example Saint Irenaeus: 'We are already that heavenly Jerusalem which was prepared and foreshadowed by the ancient city of Jerusalem'.

This then is how we should read this passage of the Council's contribution: we should avoid any rigid separation between the Church in heaven and the Church on earth; there is but *one Church* which even now is worthy of the name 'heavenly Church'.

2.   About the more immediate, historic aspects of this people of God as described in our text, I suggest two points:

— In the first instance our responsibility, as the Church, for the entire human race. We are responsible for the entirety of humanity. 'Though at times it may appear as a tiny flock, it is a most sure seed of unity, hope and salvation ... to be the instrument for the salvation of all'. We are poor, weak and ineffectual, but we have this mission in union with the whole heavenly Church. From this flows, for example, the Church's responsibility for peace which is a manifestation of the unity of the human race, and the aim of God's plan.

— In the second instance, let us consider the relationship between the historicity and the transcendence:
    'Destined to extend to all regions of the earth (the Church) enters into human history, though it transcends at once all times and all racial boundaries.'

The Church is therefore within and above; its mode of being involves being simultaneously immersed and beyond; this mode should impregnate all our actions and words — within and immersed but above. We are to be immersed but with a longer vision; we are within time but already sharing eternity; we are immersed in sufferings, emotions and struggles but at the same time in the peace of God already sharing the joy and peace of heaven.

We will return to this point when we come to a mysterious phrase of the Gospel which we are going to read.

Thus we have reflected on what 'people of God means', on what is contained in this phrase, on the responsibilities that are ours from an awareness of the Church as people of God and messianic people.

Reading from Luke: charity and politics
The text describes Jesus' attitude towards the city as a political entity. The text can be divided into three parts:

— preparation for the entry into Jerusalem;
— the description of the entry;
— Jesus weeps.

Each part is given almost equal space: the preparation at Bethphage and Bethany, the actual entry, and then Jesus' outburst of tears. The episode does not end in triumph; it ends in tears. Similarly in the verses that immediately follow — Jesus drives the traders from the Temple — the incident ends with the anger of Jesus. This is not then a glorious, idealised episode. There is a moment of glory which rapidly changes to drama.

Let us read the three parts again:

When he drew near to Bethphage and Bethany, at the mount that is called Olivet, he sent two of the disciples, saying, 'Go into the village opposite, where on entering you will find a colt tied, on which no one has ever yet sat; untie it and bring it here. If any one asks you 'why are you untying it?' you shall say this. 'The Lord has need of it'.

Two subjects dominate: *Jesus* and the *disciples* whom he tells where to go and what to answer. In this first part Jesus is in charge; he gives the orders and makes the arrangements. The two disciples only carry out these orders to the letter and all transpires as he had said.

What is the message? *Jesus is Lord.* In fact the text says 'The Lord has need of it ....' this is the first, and perhaps the only time, that Jesus refers to himself as Lord. Even in the arrangement of the details for this event he reveals himself as Lord of history; everything turns around him and is ordered toward him.

And they brought it to Jesus, and throwing their garments on the colt they set Jesus upon it. And as he rode along, they spread their garments on the road. And as he was now drawing near, at the descent of the Mount of Olives, the whole multitude of the disciples began to rejoice and praise God with a loud voice for all the mighty works that they had seen, saying, 'Blessed is the King who comes in the name of the Lord! Peace in heaven and glory in the highest!'

Jesus, Lord of history, sets off for his own city. Note the details of the narrative. The journey was from the Mount of Olives, a place replete with memories of the Hebrew people — the memory of David, of the kings and of the great events of earlier history. This is the background of memories against which the throngs of disciples, the people of God, appear.

The people of God is characterized by *praise*: it is a people that praises God with full voice. We might add to the many wonderful things said in the Council: this people enjoys the dignity and freedom of children in whose hearts the Spirit dwells, and it is characterised by its ability to praise God and recognise his marvels.

We might ask ourselves immediately: do we have this ability? As the people of God, as a parish, as a pastoral council, here in our group is our immediate characteristic, our ability to praise. Or are complaining, pessimism, fear, pettiness and quarrelling more characteristic of our behaviour?

The people sing out his praise saying: 'Blessed the king, who comes in the name of the Lord. Peace in heaven and glory in the highest!' The final words remain for me somewhat enigmatic. I hope that in speaking to you about them I may have the experience that Augustine had: in explaining the scriptures to the people he would discover the meaning of what he was about to explain.

What then is the meaning of the phrase 'Peace in heaven and glory in the highest'? What could be the reason? The expression is certainly reminiscent of the words of the angels at the birthplace of Jesus. However, in that case it was 'Glory to God in the highest and *on earth* peace' while here what is proclaimed is *'peace in heaven'*. How come this transposition, so that it would appear to be a moment of peace on earth?

It becomes even more complicated if we look at an earlier precedent for the angelic proclamation. In Isaiah 6 the cherubim sing: 'Holy, Holy, Holy, is the Lord of hosts. The earth is full of his glory'. The liturgy adds the word 'heaven' but in fact the song of the cherubim was 'the earth is full of the glory of God' for the simple reason that it was assumed that the heavens would in any case have been full of his glory. The newness is that the earth should be full of his glory.

In Luke there is a double insistence on heaven. This is the enigma. How is it that the peace which was promised on earth no longer descends on the earth? Why the emphasis on the divine dimension, on the vertical dimension of messianic peace?

My guess is — and I leave it to you to meditate on the matter — that perhaps in this instance on the eve of the passion of Jesus heaven and earth are identical; heaven comes down on the earth; the reality we already live is the heavenly reality. The heavenly Church begins here; it is one unique reality, and we contemplate the Church in this unity.

And some of the Pharisees in the multitude said to him: 'Teacher, rebuke your disciples'. He answered: 'I tell you, if these were silent, the very stones would cry out'. And when he drew near and saw the city he wept over it saying, 'Would that even today you knew the things that make for peace! But now they are hid from your eyes. For the days shall come upon you, when your enemies will cast up a bank about you and surround you, and hem you in on every side, and dash you to the ground, you and your children within you, and they will not leave one stone upon another in you; because you did not know the time of your visitation' *(Lk 19:39-44)*.

Again comment becomes difficult for there appears to be no logical reason for Jesus' weeping. The weeping is an outburst of emotion, of feeling. It is a violent eruption of contrasting feelings. We have to have experienced weeping in order to understand that there are no words to explain it. Weeping is beyond words, words do not reach those realms and so words fail to explain our tears.

Jesus weeps. He breaks out in weeping. During this night of silence we are called on to unite ourselves with the tears of Jesus, to reflect, as it were, on Jesus' *political charity* that breaks out in his heart with tears.

It must be something serious if it reaches the heart of the incarnate, Son of God and causes him to weep. The text suggests that above all Jesus weeps because there is a way to peace, a way that is open and yet it is not understood. Peace is not impossible; it is not a utopia, a pious desire. Peace is within human possibilities. Jesus is not merely speaking about peace in the sense in which it results from treaties between peoples but of that peace which is in heaven and which fills the universe. This peace is offered to humanity in the person of Jesus himself, and it is offered there and then in that visit as a wonderful gift of God. It could have been understood. It would have been enough to have recognised the visit in the mystery of Jesus' humility. But no, it was not. Jesus weeps because this historical reality, these people had gone to within one step of peace but did not know how to receive it.

Jesus weeps for history because it has been incapable of welcoming the gift of peace. At the opposite pole, the joy and thanksgiving of Jesus is recorded: 'I thank you, Father, for you have hidden these things from those who deem themselves wise and revealed them to little ones.' Then the people had reached an awareness and an experience of peace.

The Church for the life of the world

Arising from our reflection on Jesus weeping and our considerations of peace for the human family and for the civic order we can return to our initial point that the people of God is, here and now, the heavenly Church.

We are reminded of the striking insights of the Fathers of the Church — of Ambrose and Augustine — of those who lived out their faith in this very place where we are prayerfully listening to the Word of God. They were aware that the Church that gave them birth in baptism, the earthly visible Church, was at one and the same time the heavenly Church, the new Jerusalem from on high, our mother. Augustine said: 'We are now citizens of the heavenly Jerusalem; the kingdom of God has already appeared in the midst of history and peace is possible.' I would like at this point, by way of conclusion to our series of meetings to ask again the question that sometimes arises: *Is the Church for the world or, on the contrary, is the world for the Church?*

Put in these terms, the answer is clear. The Church is for the world and from this derives the Church's basic attitudes of service to humanity, and care for humanity. The Church is not an end in itself; it is at the service of a suffering humanity, an instrument of peace for humanity. Nevertheless, as St Clement of Alexandria already pointed out, that while God's will in history is called 'world', God's intention is the salvation of humanity and this is called 'Church'. In this perspective the *Church is the world reconciled.* Thus the world could be said to be for the Church because the world is called, through reconciliation, to become Church. The Church is the world reconciled, offered to the Father; the Church is the glory of God in the highest heavens but she exists and resides on earth; it is peace in heaven that is becoming peace on earth.

Hence the very serious historical obligation of the Church: she has to be above all the place where this peace and glory dwell in order to be able to testify to them, to diffuse them as the salt of the earth and the light of the world, in the phrase of *Lumen gentium* (cf. n. 9):

'Behold us, Lord, before the mystery of your Heart as we try to contemplate that Church which emerged from your transfixed Heart: the people of God and the Church concerned with the city, with social and political reality, with the unity of humanity, with peace in the world; the Church of heaven already operating here below; the Glory of God present in history; the mystery of earthly immersion and the mystery of heavenly elevation that is within, but also above history'.

It is this reality which we contemplate in the Heart of Jesus, because it is through this Heart that we share in it: here is our dignity, this is our mission, there is our call, that is the Church of which we wish to become aware.

Questions for pastoral councils

First of all there are a few questions that are addressed more specifically to members of pastoral councils. I submit them for your reflection and that of the communities.

1. Are we a people of praise? At your meetings do we begin above all with praise, thanksgiving and recognition of the gifts of God?

2. Do we remain open — even in smaller groups — to our universal obligations to history as described in the pages of *Lumen gentium*?

3. How are we helping ourselves? At this very time, on the subject of the Christian's cosmic responsibilities, the Holy Father's encyclical has appeared. It deals with the Holy Spirit and is entitled *Dominum et Vivificantem*. The cosmic dimension of Christianity is present on every page; it shows great openness to humanity's future and to the threats that endanger humanity as well as the desire and hopes of the world. Let us allow ourselves to be guided by this encyclical; allow it to open your hearts to the historic responsibilities of the people of God.

Do not be discouraged by the initial difficulties you will experience when reading it. It is somewhat difficult due to the width of the perspective which embraces the entirety of history.

Questions for youth

The first of these may well surprise you but it arises directly from the page of the Gospel that we have read:

1. Have I ever wept for my city? Have I ever wept for my community, for the persons whom I love? I know many will answer yes, even though they may, as it were, have wept inwardly. Let us try to recall those moments and relive them in union with Jesus when he wept. There is no question of a

depressed or negative weeping. Rather it is an attempt to enter into the mind of Jesus, into his way of viewing our city, into the compassion and love with which he views our cities, our history and the efforts of our communities to come to grips with the problems of our cities.

Certainly, too, we weep for ourselves and for those who are dear to us. Jesus nevertheless teaches us to weep for the city, for the world, for the suffering involved in humanity's historical journey. We should weep for our own laziness and lack of sensitivity to the suffering of humanity.

2. How shall I become involved in the ways of peace so that this, my city, which in a sense is the world, may find a way of peace? How shall I commit myself? How shall I recognise the visit of the Lord pointing to the way of peace?

We have to begin with two very simple realities. This was already suggested at last month's meeting — some gesture on behalf of the school of our diocesan mission in Kafue in Africa, and on behalf of the abandoned and suffering youth of that burgeoning city. For the future, may I suggest to you the November conference which has as its theme, 'Being a Neighbour'.

How shall I commit myself, how will I put into practice what I have learned at these Thursday meetings about the Church *for* charity, and the Church *of* charity? The meeting is but a small sign, a small visit of the Lord but we should recognise it as such in order to understand what we can usefully do to bring about peace.

'O Lord, grant that the way may not be hidden from us; grant that we may understand how in the little things of our daily lives we may welcome your visit and be at the service of peace in this city, in the world for which we frequently try to weep and for which, on this night, we pray to you, offering our sacrifices, our adoration, our silence.

Pour into our hearts, O Lord, the fullness of charity: let it be that charity which makes the suffering of one the suffering of all the members; the success of one a source of rejoicing for all. Let it be the charity that makes us aware of our being the Body of Christ and its members. Send down on us the Spirit of love and openness, of gratitude, the Spirit of patience and of peace. Unite our hearts in our proclamation and our cry: Jesus

92

is Lord! We cannot utter this cry unless in the Holy Spirit. We ask this of you, Father, through the same Jesus Christ your Son and our Lord'.